CAROL EKINSMYTH & JOHN BYNNER

THE BASIC SKILLS OF YOUNG ADULTS

SOME FINDINGS FROM THE 1970 BRITISH COHORT STUDY

A report prepared by Social Statistics Research Unit for the Adult Literacy and Basic Skills Unit (ALBSU)

ALBSU *The Basic Skills Unit*

Registered Charity No. 1003969

Acknowledgements

The project reported here was originally conceived by Professor Neville Butler, Director of the International Centre for Child Studies and founder of the 1970 British Cohort Study (BCS70) on which it is based. ALBSU agreed the terms of the contract first with ICCS and subsequently with City University when BCS70 moved to the University at the beginning of 1988. The high quality assessment materials for the project were compiled by the Cambridge Training and Development Ltd. The Advisory Group, who kept the project on course, comprised Steve Brain, ALBSU, Barbara Maughan, Institute of Psychiatry, Harvey Goldstein, Institute of Education, Mary Hamilton, University of Lancaster, David Ashton, University of Leicester, John Gray, University of Sheffield, Pat Hakim, Kingsway Further Education College and Neville Butler, International Centre for Child Studies.

Scott Montgomery of SSRU was responsible for developing the methods of the survey and overseeing the field work of which the literacy and numeracy research formed a part. He also carried out a large part of the computing and data analysis. Carol Ekinsmyth designed and organised the literacy and numeracy questioning and assessments and wrote much of the first draft of the report. John Bynner directed the project and produced the final version of the report.

Finally this report could not have been produced without the cooperation of the 1970 Cohort Study members whose continued loyalty to the study, which they have been participating in since birth, ensured its success.

© The Adult Literacy and Basic Skills Unit
7th Floor, Commonwealth House, 1-19 New Oxford Street, London WC1A 1NU.

Published February 1994

ISBN 1 870741 80 3

Design: Studio 21

Contents

Tables

Figures

Summary

1.   The 1970 British Cohort Study (BCS70) is a longitudinal study of all individuals born in the week April 5-11th, 1970, and followed up subsequently at ages 5, 10 and 16. A representative sample survey of 1,650 members of BCS70 at age 21 was carried out at the beginning of 1992.

2.   Data collection comprised an interview devoted to education, training and employment experience post-16 and self-assessed literacy and numberwork difficulties. This was followed by a half hour assessment of literacy and numeracy skills developed to operationalise ALBSU's Basic Skills Standards.

3.   Twelve percent of respondents reported problems with either reading, writing/spelling or numberwork, compared with 13% of those who reported these problems in the National Child Development Study fourth sweep of 23 year-olds in 1981 (NCDS4): three percent reported problems with reading.

4.   Although the majority of respondents had little difficulty doing most of the literacy tasks, a minority had difficulties with all of them. Poor numeracy skills were more evenly distributed across the whole population. Nineteen percent failed to get beyond Foundation level in literacy and 55% failed to get beyond this level in numeracy. Poor numeracy was related to poor literacy, but poor numeracy added another independent set of difficulties to those already present through poor literacy

5.   Common problems were reading letters and forms, working out dates and prices and keeping accounts. Specific assessment tasks which presented difficulties were interpreting complicated text, working out areas and using percentages.

6.   Poor performance in the literacy and numeracy assessment was associated with unskilled manual family backgrounds and parents who had failed to gain any educational qualifications.

7.   Respondents lacking in literacy and numeracy skills and reporting problems tended to have failed to gain any school qualifications and to have entered the labour market at the first opportunity.

8.   Male school leavers with poor literacy and numeracy tended to have spent a lot of time on training schemes, which had not led to employment, and to have experienced unemployment to a much greater extent that those without these difficulties. Females tended to stay on at school longer, to have a number of different jobs and then to exit from the labour market frequently to have children.

9.   People who reported literacy and numeracy problems had a poorer self-image than the others and tended to have experienced difficulties in education training and employment. Few had taken courses to help them with their problems.

10.   There was evidence that poor literacy and numeracy skills, as objectively assessed, had impeded educational progress and occupational success. Despite the barriers to their progress, some individuals with the deficit may not perceive a difficulty, especially as they get older and when they have managed to hold down a job without them. When they do perceive a difficulty, their self-esteem is under threat which may create psychological difficulties restricting their opportunities for employment even further.

11.   Few people who had poor basic skills, or perceived themselves to lack them, had taken advantage of the courses available to them. To maximise the numbers of people gaining assistance there is a case for more targetting within an expanded literacy and numeracy education programme to increase awareness of what is available and expand participation.

CHAPTER 1

Background to the study

1.0 Introduction

Adult literacy and numeracy problems are a central concern in modern societies. They affect not only employment prospects and the ability to perform well at work but how adults function in every area of their social and domestic lives and as citizens. Moreover, they point to serious failings of an education system which, over the years of compulsory schooling, has failed to impart the most basic of all educational skills to a proportion of children. Over the last decade programmes directed at rectifying reading and numeracy deficiencies in adults have been carried out in which the Adult Literacy and Basic Skills Unit (ALBSU) has had the main coordinating role. But the problem persists, not least because schools have yet to achieve the goal of literacy and numeracy for all the children passing through them. Nor have training schemes of the kind that burgeoned in the late 70s and the 80s bridged the gap. Gaining a better understanding of the types of problems adults have and how these develop are essential to making literacy and numeracy teaching effective.

This report examines information about literacy and numeracy that was collected at the beginning of 1992 as part of a sample survey of 1,650 21 year-olds living in England and Wales. These respondents form a 10% sample of the members of a cohort of people born between the 5th and the 11th of April 1970, and who have been studied subsequently at ages 5, 10 and 16. The 1970 British Cohort Study (BCS70) is Britain's third and youngest national longitudinal birth cohort study and follows earlier cohort studies based on samples born in 1946 and 1958 (Pringle, Butler and Davie, 1966; Butler, Golding and Howlett, 1986; Wadsworth, 1991).

The scope of the BCS70 information ranges from detailed medical examinations and histories to social background and behaviour, educational and occupational experience and educational test results. As such, the study provides a rich resource for the investigation of the extent and origins of literacy and numeracy difficulties in a young adult population.

1.1 Objectives of the study

The first objective of the study was to obtain an estimate of the proportion of English and Welsh young adults who had experienced any reading, writing, spelling or numeracy problems in their adult lives. This was, in part, directed at updating information collected eleven years previously from 23-year olds in the National Child Development Study – the cohort study based on the sample of approximately 17,000 people born in a single week in 1958 (ALBSU, 1987). Thirteen percent of the NCDS cohort members said that they had had literacy or numeracy problems since leaving school. The BCS70 survey offered the opportunity to repeat the questions in order to obtain fresh estimates and see whether there was any evidence of a marked change between the two surveys. (Such comparisons could, of course, only be crude, because of the differences in age and in the constitution of the sample between the two studies).

The second objective was to develop an assessment scheme for adult reading, writing and numberwork difficulties, which could be administered to respondents by professional survey interviewers. This would enable comparisons to be made between BCS70 cohort members' subjective appraisals of their difficulties and an objective assessment based on performance in a number of everyday tasks. The practical limitations on the design were that the assessment should take no more than 30 minutes to complete, should be simple to administer and be as enjoyable and unthreatening as possible to interviewees. The assessment needed to cover a range of performance at the four levels for communication skills and the three levels for numeracy as defined by ALBSU's Basic Skills Standards. These emphasise 'functional' performance, i.e. the ability to apply basic skills in every day life situations (ACACE, 1982).

The third objective was to investigate the kinds of difficulty people *claimed* to have and were *found* to have from the assessments. Are there particular types of task that people find exceptionally difficult and do these differ between men and women? Time limitations would of course restrict this part of the study to a very limited range of examples.

The fourth objective was to investigate the present and past circumstances and other personal characteristics of people found to have difficulties. This would bring in data from other parts of the survey and from the earlier stages of the study, exploiting its longitudinal features.

1.2 Methods

The BCS70-21 year survey collected data from 1,650 cohort members and comprised an interview and a literacy and numeracy assessment carried out by a team of professional interviewers from the MORI research organisation. Two self-completion questionnaires were also completed by respondents either before their interview, or, if they preferred, in the interview itself. The interview, which lasted on average 45 minutes, was followed by the 30 minute literacy and numeracy assessment.

1.2.1 *The Sample*

The sample of BCS70 cohort members was selected to be representative of the population of England and Wales (see Appendix 1). It involved taking first a random sample of 26 post code areas. From the list of over 10,000 up-to-date addresses for cohort members, a sample was selected in the chosen areas with probability proportional to the expected number of cohort members in the area, i.e. compensating for the differential sample loss between areas since the study began. The total sample selected in this way comprised 2,359 cohort members from which it was hoped to achieve a 70% response, i.e. at least 1,650 completed interviews.

1.2.2 *The Interview*

Besides the questions on literacy and numeracy, the interview covered a great number of other topics including educational achievement, training, employment, income, housing, social background and health. The literacy and numeracy questions were in two sets. The first set contained questions which asked respondents to assess whether or not they had any difficulties with reading, writing/spelling or mathematics. If they replied that they did have problems of some sort, they were asked the second set of questions, which attempted to discover the sort of things they had difficulty with. These questions were largely a repeat of those used in the NCDS survey (ALBSU 1987), as expanded in the recently completed fifth sweep for 33 year-olds. They are shown in the extract from the interview schedule in Appendix 2.

Self-reports to identify problems have obvious limitations for this kind of research. Because of the perceived stigma attached to illiteracy particularly, there is an incentive for respondents to disguise their reading difficulties. Another problem is that 'difficulty' is a relative concept, and one respondent's difficulty can be very different from another's. There is indeed evidence in this study that some respondents who claimed to have a difficulty, were in fact often very highly skilled in their claimed problem area, relative to the rest of the group. Many others who did not acknowledge a difficulty performed very badly on the tests. The strength of self-reports is that perception of a problem may well constitute a problem in itself. We shall also see in this study that it is the group of people who *think* that they have a problem, rather than those who we objectively discover to have a problem, who are more likely to think that they have been held back in their lives because of these difficulties.

1.2.3 The Assessment

The development of the assessments was a key part of this study. It was to be used alongside the self-reports as an objective measure of literacy and numeracy ability and as a tool to enable us to discover the sort of tasks with which people have difficulty. The combination of both self-assessment and objective assessment also enabled us to understand more about the reliability of self-assessment as a measure of literacy and numeracy. Much research in the fields of literacy and numeracy has rested on the results of such self-assessment (ALBSU, 1987). On the other hand, in the time available for the design of the study, it was not possible to undertake the developmental work necessary for the construction of a standardised test. The instrument was developed more as a device for sampling a range of tasks at different levels of difficulty from which a profile for an individual could be compiled. Although in the analysis reported here frequent use is made of overall literacy and numeracy scores obtained by aggregating scores for correct answers across the constituent items, these should be seen as no more than a means of summarising diverse data. They should not be given the status of standardised test scores.

The assessments were devised by consultants, Cambridge Training and Development Ltd., and comprised a series of tasks based around a set of everyday stimuli designed to operationalise the ALBSU Basic Skills Standards (Appendix 3). They were developed through a process of pre-testing and piloting and consisted finally of nine separate literacy tasks spanning four levels of difficulty, 10 numeracy tasks spanning three levels of difficulty, and a writing task where respondents were asked to answer in writing three further questions about their experience of doing the assessment. The results of the writing task remain to be analysed). In the case of the literacy tasks piloting showed that although the great majority of respondents could do all of them, there was a significant minority who had difficulties with all of them; a few of the tasks discriminated within the group of good readers. The numeracy tasks discriminated across the whole sample.

Interviewers' reaction to the whole assessment was favourable; it was interesting and enjoyable to administer and cohort members too appeared to enjoy doing it. On the whole, the reading tasks were preferred to the numeracy tasks, which many people admitted they found difficult. As predicted the assessment in the main field work took about 30 minutes to administer.

1.3 Field work response

The field work was carried out by the MORI research organisation. It began in January 1992 and was completed by the end of April 1992. The target total of 1,650 interviews was achieved, which as required represented over 70% of the cohort members selected for the sample. Table 1.1 gives a breakdown of the field work response.

Table 1.1: Field work response.

Outcome	%	Number
Interview	70	1650
Refusal	6	141
Moved to a different area	6	140
Moved to a new address in the same area	7	158
No contact	8	176
Incapable of doing interview	–	5
Other	4	89
Total	100	2359

The refusal rate of 6% is substantially below that of the typical cross-sectional survey and shows the continuing loyalty of cohort members to BCS70. The bulk of non-response was due to change of address and insufficient time to make contact during the period available for the survey. There are good prospects that many of these respondents will take part in future rounds of data collection.

1.4 Was the sample representative?

The sample was derived from the total up-to-date BCS70 address database in such a way as to represent as closely as possible the distribution of 21 year-olds across the regions of England and Wales. The sample excluded cohort members in Scotland because ALBSU's responsibility does not extend there. The sample was also intended to be representative of this population with respect to the main demographic characteristics such as region, sex, occupational status and marital status. In order to check the representativeness of the sample, comparisons were made with the most closely comparable data source; the 1869 21 year-olds in the 1989 national Labour Force Survey (LFS). With respect to region there were barely any differences between the two samples. Females outnumbered males (53% compared with 47%) reflecting the differential response in favour of females in BCS70 as a whole. As tables 1.2 and 1.3 show the occupational status and marital status distributions were broadly similar to those of the LFS. The BCS70 sample contained slightly more people in employment and in education than the LFS sample, which had more people unclassified in the 'other' category. This difference can be attributed largely to different coding definitions. There were also slightly more people in the 'married or cohabiting' category in the BCS70 sample. Overall the differences are sufficiently small to give us confidence that the BCS70 sample was broadly representative of 21 year-olds in England and Wales.

Table 1.2: Economic activity of 21 year-olds in BCS70 and the 1989 LFS.

Economic activity	LFS89 %	BCS70-21 %
Employed	67	70
Training scheme	1	1
Looking for work	7	10
Full-time education	9	11
Keeping house	7	7
Other	9	2
Total (100%)	1869	1650

Table 1.3: Marital status of 21 year-olds in BCS70-21 and the 1989 LFS.

Marital status	LFS89 %	BCS70-21 %
Married/cohabiting	22	26
Single	77	74
Separated/divorced	1	0
Total (100%)	1869	1650

1.5 What the project has achieved

Of the 1,650 sample members, 1,632 provided complete data on their literacy and numeracy problems and are used as the basis for the analysis reported here.

The findings suggest that literacy and numeracy problems are just as prevalent among young adults in 1992 as they were in 1981 when the comparable NCDS data for 23 year-olds was collected. Roughly 12% of the BCS70 group reported some kind of difficulty with reading, writing/spelling or numberwork or some combination of these, of which the most common was difficulty with writing and spelling. For NCDS the figure was 13%.

In addition a new assessment instrument has been developed which differentiates those with perceived difficulties from the others and also relates to many other respondent characteristics. Although much further work would usefully be done on the development of this instrument, its diagnostic value both in identifying people with difficulties at different levels and aiding understanding of the nature of their difficulties is considerable. The survey has thrown light on the critical role poor literacy and numeracy skills have in impeding progress in education and entry to the labour market. It has also shown the importance of perceived literacy and numeracy problems in affecting the course of young adults' lives, problems which do not always emerge through objective assessments. Both the objective and the subjective appraisal of difficulties are critical in understanding the functional problem and determining the best way to relieve it through teaching and counselling.

A great deal of information on literacy and numeracy has been collected, against the backdrop of information collected at earlier stages in the respondents' lives. The project potentially, therefore, has an enormous amount of analysis to draw upon, only a limited amount of which can be reported here. Further detailed work on the data will take our understanding of young adults' literacy and numeracy problems much further. For example, we shall be able to identify the family background characteristics, earlier experience in the home and the school and current attributes of people lacking basic skills, with a view to explaining how and where these skills deficits originate. Data from our other major longitudinal survey of people born in 1958 – the National Child Development Study (NCDS) – which asked at ages 23 and 33 about literacy and numeracy difficulties, can also be analysed to provide a comparative perspective across the generations.

1.6 The organisation of the report

The results of the study are reported in the next four Chapters. Chapter 2 presents the data on the prevalence of difficulties, using both the subjective and the objective assessments and, including differences between the sexes. Chapter 3 investigates the nature of the difficulties identified, and their interrelation with each other. Chapter 4 discusses the relationships between literacy and numeracy difficulties and respondents' family background and their education, training and employment. Chapter 5 discusses literacy and numeracy in relation to domestic life and psychological well-being, and participation in literacy and numeracy courses. Chapter 6 considers the policy implications of the findings.

CHAPTER 2

Who has problems?

2.0 Introduction

In this chapter we use the results of the self-reports and the assessments to estimate the prevalence of literacy and numeracy difficulties among 21 year-olds and to determine broadly what these difficulties are. The figures are also compared with those obtained for 23 year-olds in 1981 in the fourth sweep of the National Child Development Study.

2.1 The extent of literacy and numeracy difficulties?

2.1.1 The Self-reports

In the interview respondents were asked if they had any difficulties with reading, writing/spelling or numberwork (Appendix 2). If the respondent replied that they had a difficulty with any of these, the interviewer established whether this problem was due to poor eyesight, or whether it lay in failure to acquire these skills.

Table 2.1 shows that 12% (196) of respondents reported that they had difficulty of some kind with reading, writing/spelling or numberwork, of which 2% said the problem was due to eye-sight deficiency. The most common problems were with writing and spelling followed by numberwork and then reading.

Table 2.1: Self-declared reading, writing/spelling and numberwork difficulties.

Reported difficulty	Males %	Females %	Total %
Reading	5	2	3
Writing/Spelling	11	7	9
Numberwork	3	4	4
Any difficulty	14	10	12
Total (100%)	764	868	1632

The categories in Table 2.1 are not mutually exclusive. Many respondents reported that they had problems in more than one of the categories. Thus a reading problem, for example, was likely to be accompanied by writing/spelling and numberwork problems as well.

Table 2.1 also shows that males were more likely to report a basic skills difficulty than females. A greater proportion of males than females reported having difficulties with reading and writing/spelling. But for numberwork 1% *more* females than males actually reported having a problem.

The 12% reporting some kind of difficulty is close to the 13% reporting some kind of difficulty in the NCDS Survey of 23 year-olds in 1981 (ALBSU, 1987).

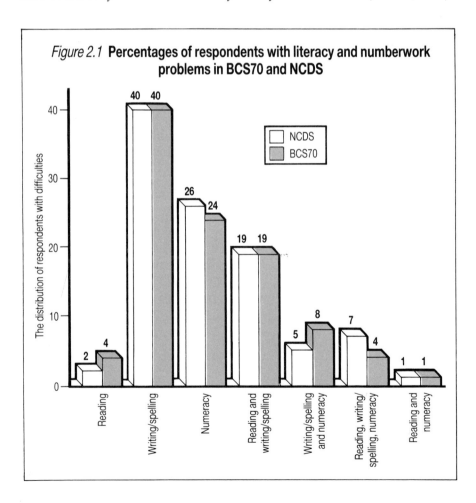

Figure 2.1 **Percentages of respondents with literacy and numberwork problems in BCS70 and NCDS**

Figure 2.1 compares the percentages of the problem group reporting different combinations of problems with the comparable percentages of NCDS respondents. It is notable that the percentages are very similar between the two surveys and that the same rank order of problems is broadly maintained. Thus writing/spelling heads the list (40%, 40%) followed by numeracy only (26%, 24%) and then reading, writing and spelling (19%, 19%). Hardly any respondents reported problems with reading only, reinforcing the point that reading problems are typically accompanied by other kinds of problem. The figures also suggest (more speculatively) that despite the efforts in schools and through programmes to improve literacy and numeracy skills in adults, the prevalence of problems, as perceived by young adults, has remained fairly constant over the ten year interval between the two surveys. The figures we have considered so far all include the 2% overall who said the basis of their problem was an eyesight deficiency. In subsequent analyses we concentrate on the group whose problems were primarily educational in origin.

2.1.3 The Assessments

As described in Chapter 1, the assessments comprised a collection of tasks that respondents were likely to come across in their everyday lives. Nine were concerned with literacy and 10 were concerned with numeracy. In this chapter we also examine some features of basic skills deficits as indicated by the summary literacy and numeracy assessment scores. These were obtained by summing responses across the individual literacy and numeracy assessment items, giving a score of 1 to each *correct* response. Thus a high literacy score was identified with a high level of literacy and a low score with poor literacy. Figure 2.2 shows the frequency distributions for the literacy and numeracy scores.

In can be seen that the literacy scores are highly skewed in the direction of high scores, whereas the numeracy scores are much more evenly spread across the whole sample. This shows, as we might expect, that poor literacy is restricted to a fairly small minority, whereas poor numeracy is a common problem. As the numbers of literacy and numeracy tasks were different, and some tasks generated more than one score, to make the summary scores comparable the raw scores were re-scaled to a range of 0-10. The re-scaled scores are used in all the analysis that follows. We shall examine the individual item responses in the next chapter.

Table 2.2 gives the means and confidence intervals for the re-scaled scores both for the assessments as a whole and at each of the Basic Skills levels as defined by the ALBSU Standards, for which assessment tasks were devised. For both

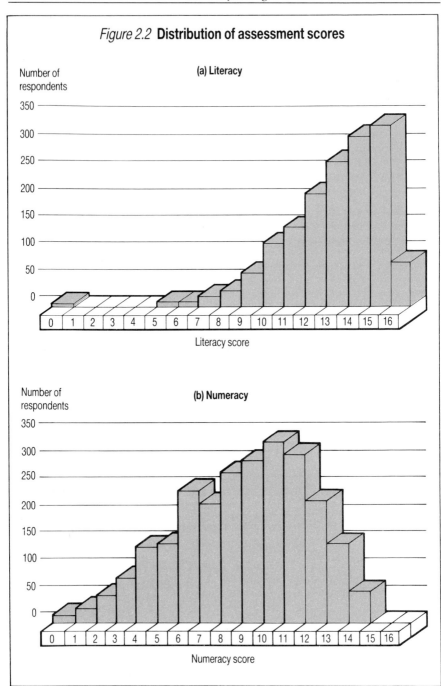

Figure 2.2 **Distribution of assessment scores**

literacy and numeracy, the Foundation tasks did correspond with the highest score (i.e. fewest people with problems). The mean scores then dropped consistently as the levels got more difficult. This suggests that the operationalisation of the ALBSU Basic Skills Standards was broadly successful.

Table 2.2: Descriptive statistics for aggregate literacy and numeracy scores.

ALBSU Basic Skills Standards	Literacy scores Mean	Confidence interval	Numeracy scores Mean	Confidence interval	Sample size (n)
Total score	7.97	0.10	5.99	0.14	1623
Foundation	9.55	0.07	8.58	0.14	1623
Level 1	8.74	0.10	5.68	0.19	1623
Level 2	5.64	0.17	4.52	0.17	1623
Level 3	2.29	0.27	–	–	1623

Note:
1. The confidence intervals given in the table are at the 1% level, i.e. the chances that the population score is approximately within the range defined by the confidence interval is 99:1. Thus the mean value of the Level 1 scores for literacy is 8.74 + or – 0.10 i.e. it lies between 8.64 and 8.84.
2. Nine cases were missing from this classification as they did not complete the assessment and thus could not be awarded a score. This reduces the sample size for analyses involving assessment scores to 1623.
3. There are four literacy levels and three numeracy levels in the ALBSU Standards.

The table also shows that this group of respondents generally performed better on the reading tasks (7.97) than the numeracy tasks (total mean score 5.99). The size of the confidence intervals for the total scores also shows that generally performance was more diverse for the numeracy tasks than for the literacy tasks. This reinforces the point made earlier that although literacy difficulties of the kind assessed are fairly rare in young adults, numeracy problems are widespread.

In order to separate out those respondents with very low as opposed to very high scores, i.e. those most lacking in the skills as opposed to those most proficient in them, respondents were classified into one of three groups. The boundaries were chosen as representing natural breaks in the distribution and where maximum discrimination between the group's characteristics and the other group's characteristics was evident. The 'low' literacy group was defined by scores in the range 0 to 5.2 (6%), the 'medium' group by scores in the range

5.3 to 9.0 (77%) and the 'top' group by scores in the range 9.1 to 10 (17%). The comparable grouping for numeracy was 'low', 0 to 3.6 (18%), 'medium', 3.7 to 7.9 (66%) and 'high', 8 to 10 (16%).

As we saw earlier, more young men than young women reported basic skills difficulties, especially those to do with literacy. For numberwork problems there was little difference between the sexes. Figure 2.3 compares the percentages of males and females in the three literacy and the three numeracy groups just defined. This time the direction of the difference was marginally reversed for the literacy scores, (6% females performed poorly compared with 5% males). For the numeracy scores there was a clear difference with more women than men falling into the low scoring group (22% compared with 13%).

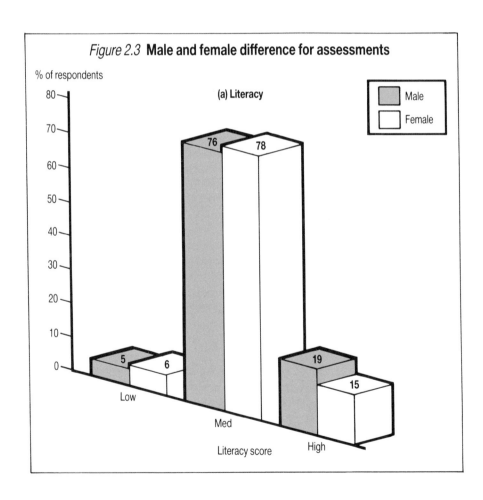

Figure 2.3 **Male and female difference for assessments**

The figures reflect the well established finding among teenage school children of greater difficulties with mathematics among girls than boys. The surprising point is that generally fewer young women appeared to acknowledge such difficulties as a problem than young men as the self-reports showed. The National Child Development Study found similar differences for self-reported difficulties. This makes a point that we shall be returning to, namely that whether a literacy or numeracy problem is perceived as important is probably more to do with its centrality to individuals in their daily lives now than the objective level of performance reached. Men care more about literacy and numeracy, presumably because of their perceived importance in work – at least at age 21. Women appear to worry less about them. It may be the case that at a later stage in their lives, when their children are of school age, for example, the

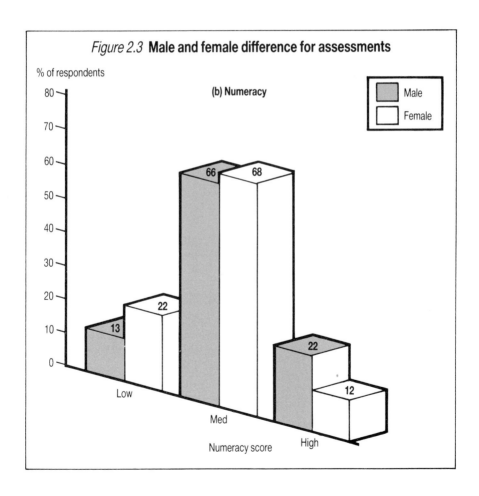

Figure 2.3 **Male and female difference for assessments**

problem takes on a new significance for women. Similarly men, as they get older, may resign themselves to a particular niche in the labour market where their poor skills can be accommodated, in which case the problem recedes.

Table 2.3 examines the low achievement group in more detail, comparing the percentages of males and females in the low scoring groups, who reported particular difficulties with reading, writing/spelling or numberwork. Twenty-two percent of males in the low literacy score group said that they had some sort of difficulty with reading and 37% had some difficulty with writing/spelling compared with 4% and 10% respectively of all respondents. The corresponding figures for females were 9% and 21% compared with 2% and 7% respectively in the total sample. It is clear therefore that males with low literacy scores were more likely to declare a problem with these skills; although the great majority of respondents who attained low scores in the literacy assessment declared *no difficulty* with either reading or writing/spelling. For numberwork problems the situation was reversed. Females who obtained low literacy scores were slightly *more likely* than males to report problems with numberwork: 13% compared with 7%.

Table 2.3: Literacy and numeracy low scores and self-assessed problems by sex.

Self-reported problems	Low literacy scores		Low numeracy scores	
	Male %	Female %	Male %	Female %
Reading	22	9	13	3
Writing/Spelling	37	21	23	11
Numberwork	7	13	26	12
Total (100%)	41	53	96	188

In the group with low numeracy scores numberwork problems were most commonly reported. But as with the low literacy score group the vast majority of respondents achieving low numeracy scores did *not* report that they had any difficulties with numberwork. This time male problems were more evident for all the skills. In confirmation of the point made earlier about the lower importance attached by the women to literacy and numeracy, it seems that in the groups genuinely lacking these skills men are generally *more* likely to see this as a problem than women. It is also clear that although the respondents in the low scoring groups are more likely than in the sample as a whole to report problems, large numbers of both sexes are either unaware of their poor skills or are aware of them but fail to acknowledge that they have a problem.

2.3 Summary and conclusion

This chapter has presented basic information about the prevalence of basic skills difficulties among BCS70-21 year-old respondents. The key findings are:

- Twelve per cent of 21-year-olds in 1992 report some reading, writing/spelling or numberwork difficulty, compared with 13% in the sample of 23 year-olds interviewed in the NCDS survey in 1981. The proportions of this group with different combinations of problems were similar in the two surveys.

- More men report having problems with reading writing and spelling than women, but for numberwork problems there is little difference between the sexes.

- Objective assessment results show highly skewed distributions for literacy scores with a minority with persistently poor performance; for numeracy the scores are far more evenly spread with large proportions of respondents unable to do most of the assessment tasks.

- Men tend to perform better on the assessments than women, especially on numeracy.

- Although the level of reporting of problems is higher in the low scoring groups than in the total sample, the great majority of people with low assessment scores do not report problems with literacy and numberwork.

In these findings we begin to see the emergence of a theme that we shall be returning to, namely that self-reported problems and objectively assessed skill deficiencies have different roles in people's lives. They need to be appraised together to gain a proper understanding of literacy and numeracy difficulties.

CHAPTER 3

What are the difficulties?

3.0 Introduction

The last chapter examined at a general level the extent of literacy and numeracy difficulties, using both the self-reports and the objective assessments, and revealed some gender differences. In this chapter we look in more detail at the nature of the difficulties people had, the kind of reading they did, and the kinds of assessment task that caused them most problems.

3.1 Self-reported difficulties

Respondents who indicated in the self-reports that they had difficulties with reading, writing/spelling or numberwork, which was not due to an eyesight defect, were asked a series of follow-on questions to discover the nature of the difficulties.

3.1.1 Reading difficulties

Three per cent of respondents (49) said they had a difficulty with reading, they were asked whether they could 'read and understand what is written in a magazine or newspaper'; 'read and understand a letter'; 'read and understand paperwork or forms'; 'read aloud from a children's story book'. Figure 3.1 shows the percentages who gave the answers 'yes', 'yes with difficulty', 'no'.

The main problems were in reading letters and forms. Over half the group said they could read personal letters and official forms only 'with difficulty' and nearly one tenth said they could not read these at all. Over a third, found difficulty reading aloud from a children's story book. Taking the answers in combination, 71% said they had difficulties with one or more of these tasks. One respondent said that, other than reading children's books with difficulty, she could not read any of the other items at all. This confirms the common finding that complete 'illiteracy' is extremely rare or at least acknowledgement of it is. Most respondents who said they had reading difficulties, were talking about fluency rather than inability to read at all.

Figure 3.1 **Reading problems**

(a) Read and understand what is written in a magazine or newspaper.

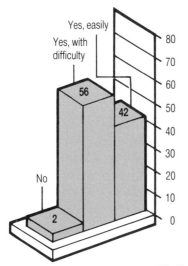

Percentage of respondents with reading difficulties.

(b) Read and understand what is written in a letter sent to you.

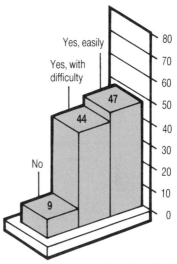

Percentage of respondents with reading difficulties.

(c) Read and understand any paperwork or forms you would have to deal with in a job.

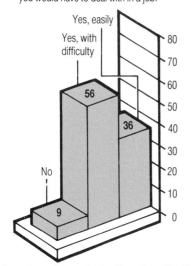

Percentage of respondents with reading difficulties.

(d) Read aloud from a children's story book.

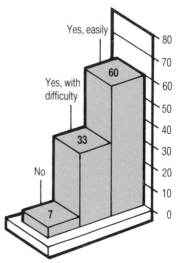

Percentage of respondents with reading difficulties.

What were the specific difficulties of this group who perceived themselves as poor readers? Figure 3.2 shows that 58% reported difficulty 'recognising words', 63% 'making sense of the whole thing' and 67% 'concentrating for very long'. Twenty nine percent reported difficulty with all of these aspects of reading, and the same proportion said they had difficulty with two of them. None of them said that they never tried to read.

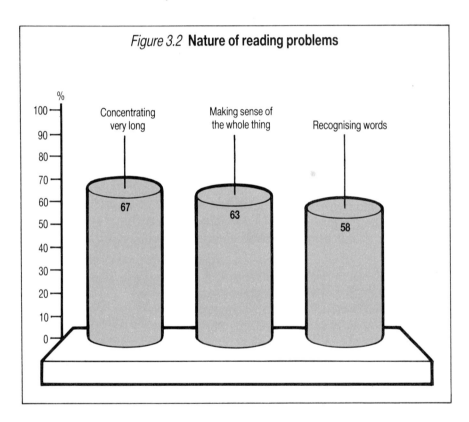

Figure 3.2 **Nature of reading problems**

3.1.2 Writing/spelling difficulties

As we saw in the previous chapter, more respondents reported that they had difficulties of some sort with writing or spelling than with any other kind of literacy tasks. The 7% who acknowledged this problem (119) were asked if they could 'write a letter to a friend', 'write a letter to an employer', 'fill in a form for the council', and 'write a letter of complaint'. Figure 3.3 gives the percentages who said they were able to perform these tasks 'easily', 'with difficulty' or 'not at all'.

Figure 3.3 **Writing problems**

(a) Write a letter to a friend to thank them for a gift or invite them to visit you.

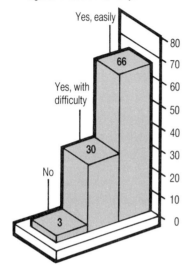

Percentage of respondents with writing difficulties.

(b) Write a letter to an employer to apply for a job.

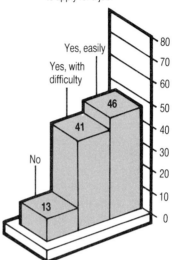

Percentage of respondents with writing difficulties.

(c) Fill in a form for the Council or for a hospital appointment.

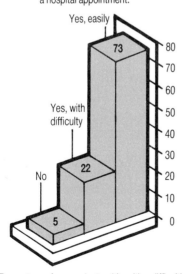

Percentage of respondents with writing difficulties.

(d) Write a letter of complaint about something.

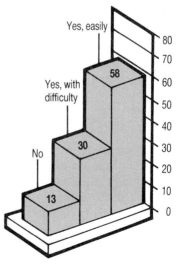

Percentage of respondents with writing difficulties.

The task that bothered most people with a writing or spelling problem was writing a letter to an employer. Just over two fifths of the group could do it only 'with difficulty', and just over a tenth said that they could not write such a letter at all. Writing a letter of complaint presented problems to a sixth who could not do it at all and about a third, who could do it only 'with difficulty'. Writing a thank you letter to a friend was difficult for much the same proportion.

Taking the answers in combination, just under two thirds of the group (64%) said they had difficulties with one or more of the tasks; 3% (3 individuals) said that they could not carry out any of them.

As for reading, respondents with a writing or spelling problem were asked about the specific difficulties they had with such tasks. Figure 3.4 shows that the great majority with problems (93%) had difficulty with 'spelling words correctly' suggesting that this is the difficulty that was worrying them most rather than writing per se; though of course, to a certain extent writing is dependent on spelling. With respect to the other difficulties, two fifths of respondents said they had difficulty writing what they 'want to say' and a quarter with making their hand-writing readable.

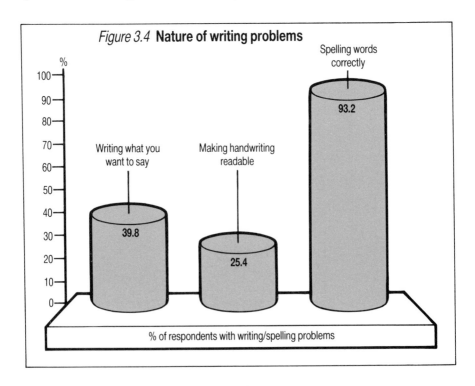

Figure 3.4 **Nature of writing problems**

Figure 3.5 **Numberwork problems**

(a) Can work out the right change from a £5 or £10 note in a shop.

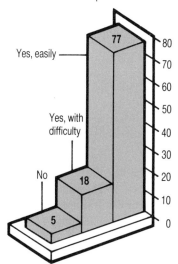

Percentage of respondents with numberwork difficulties.

(b) Can keep simple household accounts.

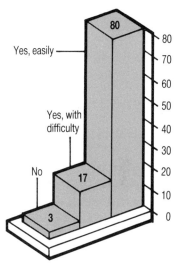

Percentage of respondents with numberwork difficulties.

(c) Can work out dates which go with which day in a calendar.

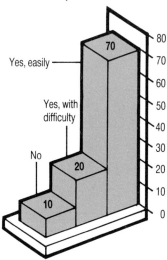

Percentage of respondents with numberwork difficulties.

3.1.3 Number difficulties

Four per cent of the total sample (65), reported that they had some sort of problem with 'numberwork'. Respondents were asked whether they could deal with three situations involving calculation 'working out whether a shopkeeper had given the right change', 'keeping household accounts' and 'working out which dates go with which days on the calendar'. Figure 3.5 show the percentages saying 'no', 'yes with difficulty', 'yes easily'.

For each task a substantial minority said they could not do it. The most difficult task appeared to be working out the dates, followed by working out the change and finally keeping household accounts. Over half the group (55%) said they had difficulty with one or more of them; 5% said they could do none of them.

These respondents were also asked if they had difficulty 'recognising and understanding numbers', 'adding up', 'taking away' and 'dividing'. Figure 3.6 shows that dividing was reported as difficult most frequently, with 70% mentioning it, followed by subtraction mentioned by just over a half, and addition mentioned by just over a third. Fourteen percent said they had

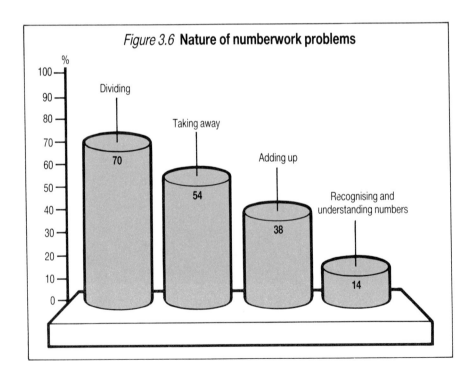

Figure 3.6 **Nature of numberwork problems**

difficulties recognising numbers. Eight percent said they found all these tasks difficult.

3.2 Literacy assessments

The Literacy Assessment consisted of 9 separate literacy tasks spanning the 4 levels of difficulty defined in the ALBSU Standards. Table 3.1 shows the percentages of males and females and of the whole sample who *failed* to complete each task successfully.

Table 3.1: Failure rates for men and women in the literacy assessment tasks.

Task	Male %	Female %	Total sample %	
Foundation				
1a	4	6	5	Interpreting a poster advertising a 'pop' concert:
1b	1	1	1	a) location b) performers
2a	3	7	5	Reading a map:
2b	6	8	7	a) quickest route b) east or west
Level 1				
3a	5	5	5	Extracting information about a restaurant from 'Yellow Pages':
3b	1	2	2	a) address b) phone number
4a	10	8	9	Interpreting a job advertisement:
4b	9	6	17	a) age limit for applicants b) how to get further information
5a	9	12	10	Extracting information from a graph:
5b	22	26	24	a) Labour's percentage of the poll b) reason for difference between graphs
5c	18	23	21	c) why Labour Party prefers graph B
Level 2				
6a	21	27	24	Interpreting the instruction manual for a video recorder:
6b	18	24	22	a) what RF is an abbreviation for b) factory setting for RF channel
6c	47	57	53	c) finding out about the Still V-lock adjustment screw
7	74	80	77	Understanding an argument in favour of hunting (giving all 4 points)
8a	48	49	48	Understanding first aid instructions for dealing with hypothermia:
8b	37	37	37	a) giving all five points b) best way to re-warm person
Level 3				
9	77	77	77	Understanding a complex literary passage (cause of Jonathan's discomfort)
Total (100%)	764	868	1634	

It is notable that for most of the tasks the failure rate was less than 25%. However, three of the tasks were beyond the reach of over half of the respondents. The most difficult tasks appeared to be understanding first aid instructions (48% failure) understanding the instructions for a video recorder (53% failure), understanding the points in an argument in favour of hunting (77% failure) and understanding a complex literacy passage (77% failure).

However the nature of the task could be just as crucial for performance as the level at which it had been placed. Thus the two level 3 tasks, which asked respondents to pick out salient points from a piece of text (7 and 8), had quite different failure rates, the former being failed by three quarters of respondents and the latter by just under a half. It appears that respondents tended to find understanding a factual text (8 – the piece on hypothermia), easier than understanding an argument (7 – the piece on blood sports). Another of the tasks which proved difficult, with over half the respondents getting it wrong (6c), required them to spot a piece of text in the top right-hand corner of a sheet taken from a video-instruction manual. In this case visual acuity may have also played a part alongside literacy in dealing with the task.

Overall the tasks designed to tap skills at the different ALBSU Basic Skills Standards appeared to be doing broadly what they were intended to do. But clearly to assess performance at the different Standards accurately, a much wider sampling of tasks in a longer assessment is needed to ensure that task-specific features do not override the literacy skills. Such an assessment would of course take much longer to do. The tasks need to be seen as indicative of literacy difficulty at different levels rather than as measures of it in a precise sense.

In the previous chapter we saw that males tended to perform slightly better overall than females on the literacy assessment, even though more males reported literacy difficulties. Table 3.1 shows that the differences could be attributed to a relatively small number of tasks. Tasks 5c, 6a, 6b, 6c, 7 all showed a difference in performance in favour of males of 5% or more. In designing these tasks it had been noted that a job advertisement (4) for the navy and interpreting the instructions on a video recorder (6) might well be more familiar and therefore found easier by men more than by women. Although the differences were small with the largest being 10% for the interpretation of the video recorder instructions, they do point to an element of gender bias which needs to be accommodated in interpreting the summary scores. But overall there is little evidence that men performed consistently better on the literacy tasks than women.

3.3 Numeracy assessments

As described in Chapter 1, the Numeracy Assessment consisted of 10 separate numeracy tasks spanning 3 levels of difficulty as defined in the ALBSU Standards. Table 3.2 shows the percentages of males and females who *failed* to complete each task successfully and of the sample as a whole.

Table 3.2: Failure rates for men and women in the numeracy assessment tasks.

Task	Male %	Female %	Total sample %	
Foundation				
10	14	16	15	Calculating change in a shop
11a	11	16	13	Working out times on a 24 hour video clock:
11b	11	20	16	a) begin recording b) finishing recording
11c	9	15	12	c) whether 4 hour tape is long enough
Level 1				
12	40	41	40	Adding 4 prices in a shop
13	59	73	67	Working out the area of a geometric shape
14	19	28	23	Working out a percentage deposit on a car price
15	40	45	43	Finding out from a table relating degree results to A level results how many subjects have more entrants with A level maths in 1979 than in 1973
Level 2				
16	75	78	76	Working out the monthly instalments on a car price
17a	20	31	26	Extracting information from a ferry timetable about cost of travel in August:
17b	44	54	50	a) dates for cheapest travel; b) total return cost for two people by car
18a	87	93	90	Working out discount prices on two jackets in a sale:
18b	36	47	42	a) working out difference in price; b) deciding which jacket is cheaper
19	36	78	48	Finding out from a table relating degree results to A level results what percentage of the students did engineering and technology in 1973
Total (100%)	764	868	1634	

Reflecting the wider spread of numeracy scores, which we saw in the previous chapter, far fewer respondents were able to handle the individual numeracy tasks than was the case for the literacy tasks. Although at the Foundation Level less than one fifth were defeated by them, at the higher levels the failure rates ranged from 23% to 90% with the majority of tasks having failure rates of over 40%. There was also evidence of even greater diversity of response at each level and between levels than for literacy, which points again to task-specific features overriding the numeracy assessment.

Thus at Level 2, task 17a, comprising the interpretation of a ferry timetable, was failed by one quarter of respondents. In contrast, as many as three quarters failed task 16 and nine tenths 18a, which involved respectively working out monthly payments on a car purchase loan and a more complex conversion of percentages into prices. Such tasks were clearly a problem for substantial numbers of people. Adding prices together, a Level 1 task (12), not unexpectedly was less difficult, even though two fifths failed to do it correctly. Another Level 1 task, calculating the area of a geometric shape (13), was beyond the great majority of people; two thirds were unable to do it.

As we saw in chapter 2, there were larger differences in the mean total scores between men and women for numeracy than for literacy, with men having the higher mean score. Again the large differences were concentrated in a few of the tasks. Calculating the area of a shape (13), proved exceptionally difficult for women, with three quarters of women failing to manage it compared with three fifths of men. Reading a table of figures (19) was also substantially more difficult for women with 42% more women than men failing to do it. Differences in the order of 10% in favour of men occurred for working out a percentage (14), working out the cheapest fare and the cost of tickets from the ferry timetable (17a and 17b) and deciding which of two jackets was cheaper in price (18b).

Interpreting these differences is more difficult than for the literacy scores. As with literacy there is clearly an element of gender bias in items which functionally are, perhaps, more familiar to men. On the other hand, it could be argued that in practice they are equally functionally important for both men *and* women, which suggests that women have a particular problem with these kinds of tasks that needs to be tackled.

3.4 ALBSU Standards

Can we use performance on the individual tasks at different levels to gain an indication of the percentages of young adults failing to achieve ALBSU's Basic Skills Standards? For the reasons stated earlier, such estimates are contingent on the particular tasks sampled to assess standards at a given level; therefore how generalisable the estimates are depends on how representative the selected tasks are of the ALBSU Basic Skills Standards. Moreover we have to assume that a single dimension with gradations of difficulty is being tapped by the tasks; failure to do tasks at Level 1 implies failure to do them at Level 2 and so on. We took as a definition of passing tasks at a particular level, success with half or more of them.

On this basis we can conclude that in our sample of 21 year-olds for literacy averaging across the tasks at each level, 13% were below Foundation Level; 6% were at Foundation but below Level 1; 32% were at Level 1 but below Level 2; 36% were at Level 2 but below Level 3. Only 12% had passed all four literacy levels. For numeracy we have a worse picture at the bottom and a better one at the top because the Standards for numeracy contain only three levels. 20% had failed the tasks at the Foundation Level; a further 35% had failed to get beyond Foundation Level; and 19% had failed to get beyond Level 1. This means that only 25% had passed all three numeracy levels.

3.5 Relation between types of self-reported difficulty and assessment tasks

In the previous chapter we saw that the literacy and numeracy total scores obtained by aggregating responses over all the assessment items were related to self-reported problems. To what extent does this relationship extend to the individual assessment tasks?

Table 3.3 shows the percentages of all respondents in the total sample giving the correct answer to each of the literacy assessment items and in the groups with each of the three types of self-declared problem, reading, writing/spelling, numberwork. Respondents with self-declared problems fared worse in the assessment tasks compared with the total sample of respondents. This was particularly the case for the 'reading problems' group; but, especially at the more advanced levels. It also applied to the 'writing/spelling problems' group and even the 'numberwork problems' group. This reinforces the point made in the previous chapter that literacy and numeracy problems are inter-related, and indeed, it is often difficult to separate the two skills. Thus, all numerical tasks require a degree of literacy in order to understand them, and in the case of some, such as extracting information from a timetable or interpreting a table of figures, a large component of literacy may be involved.

Table 3.4 shows the percentage of all respondents in the total sample giving the wrong answer to each of the numeracy assessment items in the groups with each of the three types of self declared problem, reading, writing/spelling, numberwork. Again, we see that literacy problems (reading and writing/

Table 3.3: Failure rates for the literacy assessments tasks related to self-declared problems.

Task	All respondents %	Self-reported problems		
		Reading %	Writing/Spelling %	Numberwork %
Foundation				
1a	5	16	12	7
1b	1	14	4	3
2a	5	16	10	5
2b	7	18	9	5
Level 1				
3a	5	27	22	9
3b	2	9	5	3
4a	9	23	16	14
4b	17	41	36	29
5a	10	23	22	26
5b	24	29	34	36
5c	21	32	32	31
Level 2				
6a	24	48	40	34
6b	22	54	44	33
6c	53	66	62	57
7	77	81	84	81
8a	48	73	67	67
8b	37	77	51	50
Level 3				
9	77	93	81	72
Total (100%)	1634	44	115	58

spelling) are likely to be as significant in poor numeracy as numberwork problems themselves. For the three tasks, 12, 14, and 15, which were concerned with adding four prices in calculating a percentage and extracting information from a table, the proportion of respondents getting the wrong answer was actually *lower* among the group with numberwork problems than the group with reading problems.

Table 3.4: Failure rates for the numeracy assessments tasks related to self-declared problems.

Task	All respondents %	Self-reported problems		
		Reading %	Writing/Spelling %	Numberwork %
Foundation				
10	15	26	26	34
11a	13	23	22	23
11b	16	16	18	29
11c	12	11	15	23
Level 1				
12	40	53	49	52
13	67	81	83	86
14	23	61	48	57
15	43	76	59	67
Level 2				
16	75	90	92	100
17a	26	37	41	41
17b	50	63	61	71
18a	90	93	97	100
18b	42	57	63	63
19	48	85	71	81
Total (100%)	1634	44	114	58

Overall though, much the same picture emerged as for literacy: poor performance on the numeracy assessment tasks was substantially more prevalent among the problem group than in the total sample. For example, of the respondents with self-declared numberwork difficulties, nobody could calculate monthly repayments on a car over 3 years (16), and nobody could convert a percentage discount into a price (18a). 86% could not work out the area of a shape (13) and 81% could not calculate a percentage from a table of figures (19).

3.6 The relationship between literacy and numeracy difficulties

Can literacy and numeracy skills be separated and independently assessed in functional terms? We have observed already in this chapter that respondents exhibiting low skills or reporting problems for literacy also tended to have low skills and problems in numeracy. It would appear that respondents with numeracy difficulties were more likely also to experience literacy difficulties rather than the other way round. In other words, numeracy skills are to a certain extent dependent on literacy skills. They also add another (independent) set of problems to those that are already present. This of course makes perfect intuitive and educational sense; we need to learn the vocabulary of mathematics before we can practise it, so learning to read is given greater emphasis in education.

The relationship between the results of the self-assessments and the objective assessments is clearly not a straight-forward one. Reporting a difficulty depends on a number of factors, not least the importance of the skill to the individual. This can mean that somebody who works with words all the time such as a journalist may still feel they have further to go to become a good writer. In contrast, somebody in a manual job may need only minimal literacy skills in the work they do and be quite happy with the level of skill they have. Writing and spelling is particularly prone to this kind of 'relative appraisal'. Most professional jobs, for example, involve a lot of writing so very high standards may be set by the individual in their performance of their job. Indeed, we have already seen in Chapter 2 that some respondents said that they had difficulties and then answered that they could perform 'well' all the activities asked about subsequently. The shortcomings of the self-reports is that we don't know the *standards* that respondents are comparing themselves to. The advantage of the objective assessments is that they enable us to pin down more precisely the difficulties people actually have against a common set of standards. As we shall see in the next chapter, however, this does not necessarily mean that the objectively assessed problem is always more important than the self-perceived problem to the people who have it. Both kinds of appraisal are essential to understand the remedial help adults need.

3.7 Summary and conclusions

This chapter has unravelled the nature of literacy and numeracy difficulties in more detail. We have examined the kinds of problems people report having and have used the literacy and numeracy assessment tasks to discover more objectively what kinds of difficulties existed.

We can conclude that:

- Self-reported reading difficulties are concentrated on understanding forms and letters: over half report doing these only with difficulty.

- Self-reported writing/spelling problems are mainly about spelling and being able to express oneself: two thirds report having difficulty with these.

- Self-reported numberwork difficulties are spread between working out change, keeping accounts and working out dates: one half report not being able to do one of these.

- Although many of the literacy tasks are easy for the majority of people, for interpreting graphs, understanding instructions and arguments and a complex piece of literary text failure rates reach over 50%.

- Failure in the numeracy tasks is more widespread than for the literacy tasks with failure rates exceeding 40% for a majority of them.

- Females' poorer performance on some literacy assessment items can be attributed to the items' greater familiarity to males, but the consistently poorer performance among females across all the numeracy assessment items points to a real skills deficiency among them.

- There is evidence that substantial proportions of young adults are unable to pass the 4 Literacy levels and the 3 Numeracy levels in the ALBSU Basic Skills Standards: 88% failed to reach literacy level 3 and 80% had failed to reach numeracy Level 2.

- People with self-reported literacy and numeracy problems tend also to perform poorly on literacy and numeracy tasks respectively, but quite large proportions who perform badly do not acknowledge any problem.

- Literacy and numeracy skills and problems overlap, with poor literacy underpinning poor numeracy, and poor numeracy adding a further set of problems.

Although the same people tend both to report difficulties and to perform badly on the assessments, substantial numbers reveal a problem in one situation and not in the other. There are indications that the self-reports are more concerned with standards of difficulty relative to everyday experience than the assessment tasks which give a more objective appraisal of performance against common standards. As we shall see in the next chapter, the former may, in fact, be as important to the individual, especially in releation to the work they do.

CHAPTER 4

Basic skills and working life

4.0 Introduction

In the previous two chapters we considered the extent of literacy and numeracy difficulties and what the difficulties are. This chapter presents findings relating literacy and numeracy difficulties to the areas of cohort members' lives where we might expect the impact to be greatest: progress first in education and subsequently in the labour market. We start by examining some features of the family backgrounds of those with these problems.

4.1 Social background

4.1.1 Social class

Literacy and numeracy difficulties start early in life, which means that family circumstances are critical in understanding how they occur. The BCS70 longitudinal data enable us to relate current numeracy and literacy difficulties to home background earlier on in the cohort members' lives. The age 10 data were judged to be the most reliable and appropriate for this purpose. Table 4.1 shows the percentages of respondents from each of the six social classes defined by the Registrar General's classification of fathers' occupation who fell into the 'low' literacy and numeracy score groups defined in the last chapters, or reported basic skills problems.

As we might expect, the respondents in the low literacy score and low numeracy score groups tended to come from the unskilled and semi-skilled social classes. There was a steady *increase* in the percentage with *low* scores going from social class I (professional) to social class V (unskilled) homes. This was notably, much more marked for numeracy than for literacy. Half the cohort members from unskilled families were in the low numeracy score group but only one sixth were in the low literacy score group. There are many complicating factors in interpreting this relationship. For example, is it the level of literacy in the home that is critical or is it the way class manifests itself through schooling? Nevertheless the figures underline the connection between children's social circumstances and their later development.

Table 4.1: Family social class and literacy and numeracy scores and self-assessed problems.

	Prof. (I) %	Inter. (II) %	Skilled N.M. (III) %	Skilled Manual (III) %	Semi-Skilled (IV) %	Unskilled (V) %	Total %
Low literacy scores	2	2	3	8	6	15	5
Low numeracy scores	8	8	9	20	25	48	17
Self-reported reading problems	4	2	2	2	1	10	2
Self-reported writing/spelling problems	12	5	5	7	7	8	6
Self-reported numberwork problems	6	3	5	4	1	5	4
Total (100%)	50	259	120	429	142	40	1040

Note: NM = Non-manual

A rather different picture was apparent for the self-assessed problems. Across all the classes the percentages reporting problems was relatively low usually at around 5%. However, in the case of reading problems, 10% of the unskilled group said they had the problem and in the case of writing and spelling the top percentage was 12% in the professional group. Here we see the probable effect of relative standards in self-assessment. It seems likely that the professional families set subsequently higher literacy and numeracy standards for their children than do the other social class groups; hence the higher than average perception of problems in this group.

4.1.2 Parents' educational attainment

Family social class to a certain extent reflects parent's own performance in the education system. The standard they achieved adds the educational dimension to the social characteristics and lifestyle of the home, which again might be expected to play an important role in the development of literacy and numeracy skills in the children. Parents' educational attainment, reported when the cohort members were aged 10, was based on the highest school and post-school qualifications achieved by one or other parent, classified on a five point scale ranging from 'no qualifications' to 'a degree'. Figure 4.1 shows the percentages of cohort members with 'low' literacy and numeracy scores respectively in each of the five parental attainment groups.

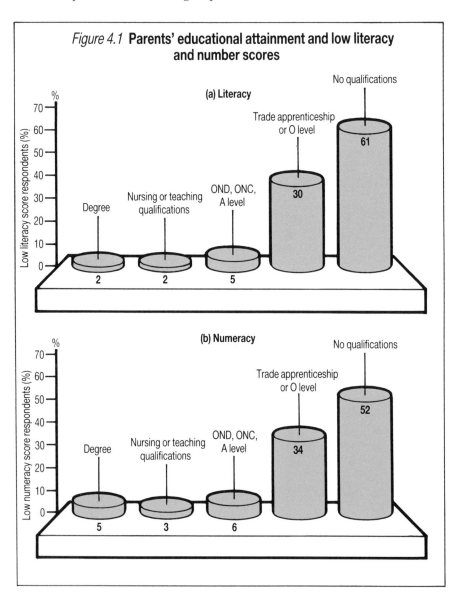

Figure 4.1 **Parents' educational attainment and low literacy and number scores**

The differences are striking. Three fifths (61%) of respondents with parents in the bottom attainment group had low literacy scores compared with only 2% in the highest parental attainment group. Differences for numeracy were also evident but on a smaller scale. Thus just over half (52%) of the bottom parental attainment group contained cohort members with low numeracy scores compared with only 5% of the top group. These relationships between poor literacy and numeracy performance and family background were just as strong in both sexes. This points to a degree of family disadvantage lying behind both men and women's subsequent literacy and numeracy difficulties.

4.2 Educational attainment

4.2.1 School examination achievement

We would expect to find that the characteristic with the closest connections to respondents' adult literacy and numeracy would be their own educational attainment. Without literacy and numeracy skills the whole of an educational career is stunted; hence in some respects the adult literacy and numeracy difficulties may be seen as manifesting both the seeds of and the culmination of a life time of educational failure. After leaving school the problem is brought home in particularly stark form, because further educational progress as an adult is effectively prevented if literacy and numeracy skills are lacking. Table 4.2 relates membership of the three literacy and numeracy groups to school level educational attainment.

Table 4.2: Respondents' school qualifications and literacy and numeracy scores.

| Highest qualifications | Literacy scores | | | Numeracy scores | | | All respondents |
	Low %	Medium %	High %	Low %	Medium %	High %	%
None	38	9	2	25	8	2	10
1-5 CSEs*	39	27	7	39	26	6	24
1-4 O Levels	21	37	24	30	38	23	34
5+ O Levels	3	15	19	4	16	25	16
A Levels	0	11	47	2	13	45	17
Total (100%)	88	1213	274	269	1044	262	1575

Note: *Grade 2 or below

Two-fifths (38%) of cohort members in the low literacy score group had not achieved any academic qualifications at school compared to 2% of the high literacy assessment group. Three quarters of the low literacy group (77%) had achieved *less* than 5 CSE's of grade 2 or below. None had achieved A Levels compared with 47% in the high literacy group.

For the numeracy group we find a similar but weaker relationship. A quarter of cohort members with low numeracy scores had not achieved any formal qualifications at school, as opposed to only 2% of the high numeracy group. Just under half the high numeracy group had achieved 'A' levels but perhaps more surprisingly so had 2% of the low numeracy group. This demonstrates the more specialised nature of numeracy skills. Clearly high levels of achievement in the English education system are not necessarily impeded by poor numeracy, whereas literacy is fundamental to success.

Table 4.3 extends the picture, comparing the percentages of males and females with qualifications in the low score groups and among those with self-reported problems and in the total sample. Performance for both sexes in the low score groups was much worse than in the total sample. However, in addition the males with low literacy scores had performed worse than their female counterparts. 44% of the young men in this group had no formal qualifications compared with 33% of the young women.

Table 4.3: Respondents' school qualifications and literacy and numeracy scores and self-assessed problems by sex.

Highest qualifications	Literacy scores		Numeracy scores		Reading		Self-reported problems writing/spelling		Number		All respondents	
	Low	Low	Low	Low								
	M %	F %	M %	F %	M %	F %	M %	F %	M %	F %	M %	F %
None	44	33	32	22	25	50	22	30	32	17	10	9
1-5 CSEs	38	38	37	40	32	28	40	32	37	32	26	22
1-4 O Levels	15	24	29	30	36	21	31	26	19	28	33	35
5+ O Levels	3	4	3	5	4	0	1	8	5	6	14	16
A Levels (A-E)	0	0	0	3	4	0	6	2	9	17	16	17
Total (100%)	39	49	89	180	28	14	69	43	22	35	735	834

As with literacy, males in the low numeracy group performed worse in their school examinations than their female counterparts. A third of the males in this category had achieved no formal qualifications at school as opposed to only a fifth of the females.

We can only speculate about the reasons for these male-female differences. We saw in Chapter 2 that women performed overall slightly worse than men on both the literacy and the numeracy assessments, which could be attributed in part to a slight gender bias, at least in the literacy assessment. This would affect the differences in the direction we have found, but only slightly. What seems more likely is that subject choice and anticipated post-school destination has something to do with the differences. It may be that girls with poor basic skills take subjects that are easier to pass. Boys lacking basic skills are already more set on leaving school at the earliest minimum age which makes examination success less important to them. In common with other surveys and the national statistics on school leaving, a higher percentage of men in the sample (51%) left full-time education at 16 than women (44%).

With respect to self-reported problems some of the relationships found previously were reversed (Table 4.3). Half the women who said that they had problems in reading had achieved no school qualifications, compared with only a quarter of the men. Clearly, although low skills, as assessed objectively, had been *less* of a problem in gaining qualifications for women than for men, women who reported having a reading problem appeared to have had *more* difficulty in gaining qualifications. In this case the perceived importance of the skill, in relation to the subjects women wanted to succeed in, was probably crucial. *Fewer* women than men with numberwork problems had failed to obtain any qualifications – again perhaps a reflection of the lower importance attached to numeracy in the subjects women study.

4.2.2 Post-school achievement

Figure 4.2 shows the percentages who had achieved any kind of post-school qualifications in each of the three literacy groups and the three numeracy groups. Half the respondents had achieved a post school qualification. Those who had performed badly in the literacy assessment were far less likely to have gained a qualification than those who had performed well (23% compared with 64%). A similar but weaker relationship was also evident for numeracy (37% compared with 62%) again showing that poor numeracy is less of an impediment to educational achievement than poor literacy. Four percent of the low numeracy score group had actually achieved a degree!

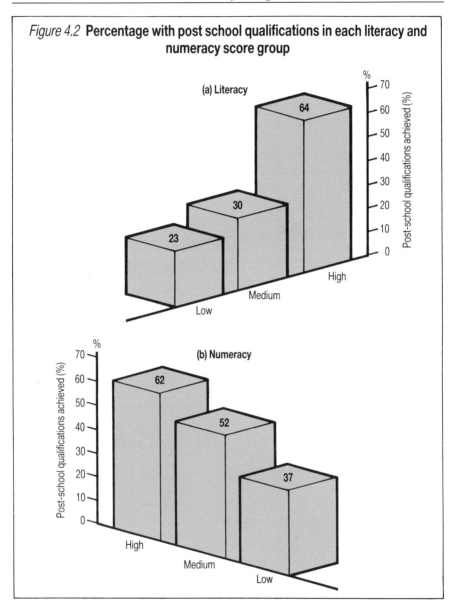

Figure 4.2 **Percentage with post school qualifications in each literacy and numeracy score group**

Table 4.4 opposite shows the types of qualification achieved by men and women in the low score groups and the self-reported problem groups and in the total sample. The most common kind of qualifications were vocational (RSA, CGLI, BTEC) of which CGLI was the most frequently reported.

In contrast to school qualifications, for post-school qualifications women in the problem groups had done consistently worse than men. For example, 65% of women with low numeracy scores had not achieved any post-school qualification compared with 59% of men. It seems that at this stage women's awareness of a difficulty is translated more frequently into a decision to opt out of qualifications, than is men's – a reflection perhaps of the reduced significance of qualifications in these women's lives.

Table 4.4: Respondents' post school qualifications and literacy and numeracy scores and self-assessed problems by sex.

Highest post-school qualification	Literacy scores		Numeracy scores		Reading		Self-reported problems writing/spelling		Number		All respondents	
	Low	Low	Low	Low								
	M	F	M	F	M	F	M	F	M	F	M	F
	%	%	%	%	%	%	%	%	%	%	%	%
None	76	77	59	65	57	79	47	67	48	63	47	51
O/A Levels	2	2	3	1	0	0	1	2	4	4	3	4
RSA/CGLI/ TEC/BEC	21	29	35	28	40	21	44	22	35	21	36	29
Professional	0	2	1	1	3	0	4	2	9	6	3	5
University/ Polytechnic	0	0	1	5	0	0	4	7	4	6	11	11
Total (100%)	41	53	96	188	30	14	72	43	23	23	759	864

We have seen in this section that literacy and numeracy difficulties were evident in earlier educational attainment. Adults with literacy difficulties were less likely to have succeeded in school examinations and were less likely to have achieved post school qualifications. Were they also more likely to leave education at 16 and what happened to them if they left?

4.3 Transition from education to employment

At 16 young people have the option of staying on in education or leaving and within these options a number of further choices are open to them. At the time the cohort members were facing post-16 choices, training schemes (YTS – the Youth Training Scheme for instance) were replacing direct entry into jobs for large numbers of school leavers, and many young people who refused to enter or failed to gain entry to the schemes experienced unemployment. Following the classification used in ESRC's 16-19 Initiative which studied the same age group at much the same time (Bynner, 1989; Banks et al, 1991), six post-16 broad occupational routes or 'career trajectories' were defined:

- Academic – staying on a purely academic path between the ages of 16 and 18, taking 'A' levels

- Non-academic – continuing in education after the age of 16, but for vocational purposes

- Education to work – direct entry into a job at 16

- YTS to work – 'two step' transition into a job, via YTS after leaving school

- YTS – still involved in a training scheme at 19

- Mixed – mixture of jobs, training and education interspersed typically with unemployment.

We might expect literacy and numeracy difficulties to be closely connected with entry into these routes. Those with difficulties would be less likely to stay on in education than the others and more likely to enter training schemes.

Table 4.5 compares the distributions across the six trajectories for each of the literacy and numeracy groups.

Table 4.5: Career trajectory and literacy and numeracy scores.

Career trajectory	Literacy scores			Numeracy scores			All respondents %
	Low %	Medium %	High %	Low %	Medium %	High %	
Staying On Academic	0	10	46	2	12	43	15
Vocational	18	24	22	19	25	23	24
Leaving Job	27	27	14	23	26	21	25
YTS-Job	17	13	6	17	13	4	12
YTS	18	15	6	22	13	6	14
Mixed	20	11	6	17	11	4	11
Total (100%)	94	1252	277	284	1074	265	1623

The figures confirm our expectations, but only to a certain extent. With the exception that hardly anybody in the low literacy or numeracy groups had stayed on in education on the academic route to take 'A' levels, the distribution across the other trajectories for this group was relatively even. In contrast, among the high literacy and numeracy groups, approaching half were on the academic trajectory. The low achievement groups were also much more likely to have gone straight from school to work, to have entered YTS programmes and still be on these at the age of 19, or to be on the 'mixed' trajectory. From their earliest post-school days, therefore, the low literacy and numeracy groups appeared to have been experiencing the more difficult and less secure options in the world of work and training, leaving school early, and finding jobs or YTS or becoming unemployed, depending on the strength of the local economy.

As we noted earlier, male and female occupational careers differ, so we might expect to find further differences in the career trajectory relationships examined for men and women separately. Table 4.6 compares the percentages of males and females in different career trajectories for the low-assessment score groups.

Table 4.6: Career trajectory and literacy and numeracy scores and self-assessed problems by sex.

Career trajectory	Literacy scores		Numeracy scores		Reading		Self-reported problems writing/spelling		Number		All respondents	
	Low	Low	Low	Low								
	M %	F %	M %	F %	M %	F %	M %	F %	M %	F %	M %	F %
Academic	0	0	0	3	3	0	6	2	4	17	15	16
Vocational	15	21	14	21	3	43	8	30	26	26	18	29
Job	32	23	28	20	23	14	28	12	26	9	30	20
YTS-Job	15	19	15	19	20	14	17	9	13	9	12	12
YTS	27	11	31	18	37	14	28	19	22	14	16	11
Mixed	12	26	14	19	13	14	14	28	9	25	9	12
Total (100%)	41	53	96	188	30	14	72	43	23	23	759	864

Although in the total sample roughly equal proportions of males and females had followed the 'academic' trajectory, more females than males were to be found on the 'vocational' trajectory, and more males than females had gone straight from school to a job. The differences between males and females were repeated in the low literacy and numeracy score groups. Disproportionately more of the males in these groups were to be found on the 'YTS' trajectory and more of the females were to be found on the 'mixed' trajectory. This analysis shows that both males and females in these low-ability groups appear to be suffering disadvantage in the workplace, but they respond differently to them. Males are more likely to participate in training programmes that do not lead immediately to work, and females are more likely to try a number of things without settling into a clear trajectory at all, or leaving the labour market altogether.

Self-declared problems presented a similar picture to the assessments which is interesting because we have already seen that the people with these problems were not necessarily the same as those who were 'below average' in ability terms as defined by the results of the objective assessment. Could it be that some of these individuals had low self-esteem and dared not allow their aspirations to outstrip what they regarded as their ability. They had thus ended up in more disadvantaged positions than they needed to?

4.4 Unemployment

Among the early school leavers, experience of unemployment was a common phenomenon. Those who had entered YTS schemes, for example, had frequently been unemployed first and the group on the 'mixed' trajectory contained a large number who had been unemployed, for some for most of the period since leaving school. With respect to current occupational status, higher proportions of those in the low literacy and numeracy groups and among those reporting problems said that they were currently unemployed (Table 4.7). Unemployment was particularly prevalent for males and highest of all among those with self-reported numeracy problems (39%). Females with low literacy or numeracy scores or with self-reported problems tended to be engaged in 'housecare' rather than to be unemployed.

That unemployment at the time of interview was not a temporary state but a relatively permanent feature of early careers for many in these groups is shown by relating length of time unemployed (and looking for work) since leaving school and poor literacy and numeracy.

Figure 4.3 shows the mean numbers of months unemployed for men and women separately in each of the literacy and numeracy groups and in the groups defined by self-reported literacy and numeracy problems.

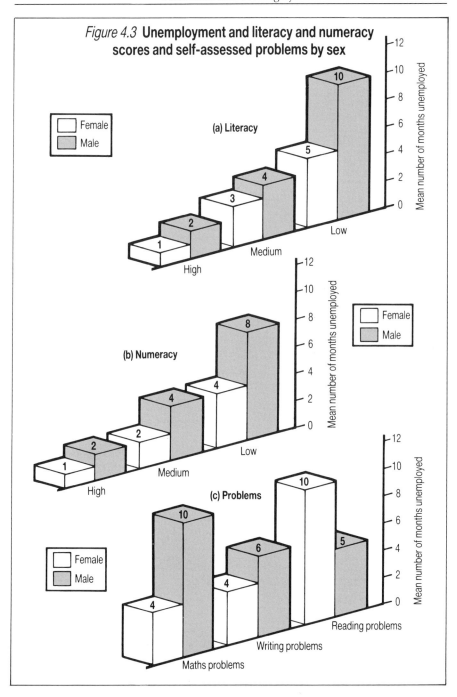

Figure 4.3 **Unemployment and literacy and numeracy scores and self-assessed problems by sex**

(a) Literacy

(b) Numeracy

(c) Problems

Table 4.7: Unemployment at time of interview and literacy and numeracy scores and self-assessed problems by sex.

	Literacy scores		Numeracy scores		Reading		Self-reported problems writing/spelling		Number		All respondents	
	Low M %	Low F %	Low M %	Low F %	M %	F %	M %	F %	M %	F %	M %	F %
Unemployment	35	8	25	7	10	14	18	12	39	11	13	6
Housecare	0	34	2	22	0	29	1	26	0	20	0	12
Training	2	4	4	2	0	0	3	0	0	0	1	1
Total (100%)	41	53	96	188	30	14	72	34	23	35	759	864

The critical importance of literacy and numeracy skills in getting jobs and keeping them is apparent, but especially for men. Five times more months of unemployment had been experienced by low literacy men compared with high literacy men and similarly for low literacy women, five times as much as for high literacy women. Broadly, as literacy skills increased unemployment went down. Much the same picture applied for numeracy but the relationship was weaker in both sexes. Interestingly, the time women had spent unemployed in each of the literacy and numeracy groups was also substantially below that for men: overall, women had spent half the time unemployed that men had experienced. This is probably a feature of the different relationship women have to the labour market, particularly those with poor attainments at school. Although women are more often to be found than men in clerical occupations apparently requiring literacy skills, those without them, are more likely to be at home and out of the labour market.

This might appear to reduce the significance of literacy and numeracy difficulties in women's employment but this is not the case. With respect to *self-reported* literacy problems, it was the women who had them who had experienced the most unemployment. For men it was problems with numberwork which appeared the most critical.

This is a good example of the different role the objective and the subjective elements of literacy and numeracy difficulties play in people's lives. In women's favoured occupations verbal skills are more at a premium than maths skills; hence perceived lack of them weakens confidence in getting jobs and being accepted for them, an aspect, perhaps, of reduced self-esteem. The reverse applies for men: maths skills, at least as perceived, are more at a premium. Lack of skills, as assessed objectively, reflects a generally poor educational level which relegates men to unskilled manual occupations. It was in these areas of the labour market where unemployment in the late 80s was highest; hence the problem these young men had with finding and holding on to a job. In other words men were being forced into unemployment because they lacked skills. Women were opting out of desired female occupations into unskilled (often part-time work) and unemployment because of a *perceived* lack of skills.

4.5 Summary and conclusion

The findings presented in this chapter suggest that the precursors of literacy and numeracy difficulties and the personal characteristics that accompany them are numerous and heavily inter-related. Accumulated disadvantage at home and subsequently through education gives way to poor employment prospects underpinned by lack of basic skills. We can conclude that:

- Poor adult literacy and especially poor adult numeracy are associated with unskilled family backgrounds in which the parents have failed to gain any educational qualifications.

- Adults who lack literacy and numeracy skills and report literacy and numberwork problems achieve poorly at school and few gain any qualifications afterwards.

- Men with poor literacy and numeracy skills enter the labour market early and experience training schemes and unemployment; women with literacy and numeracy difficulties tend to leave the labour market early.

A picture emerges of the person lacking basic skills as being marginalised first in education and then in the peripheral unskilled regions of the labour market, typically with long spells of unemployment. In the case of women, the response to employment difficulties is frequently an exit from the labour market into 'housecare'.

CHAPTER 5

Basic skills and personal life

5.0 Introduction

We have seen in the last chapter that men and women with literacy and numeracy problems tend to come from disadvantaged family backgrounds and to make poor progress in the education system and in the labour market. There was evidence of higher unemployment among men and a greater tendency for women to be out of the labour market. To what extent were these differences carried over into personal life and into psychological well-being and what attempts had been made to do something about them?

5.1 Domestic circumstances – marriage, children

There is no obvious reason why literacy and numeracy difficulties should have an effect on domestic life, especially the decision to get married or cohabit and have children. If there is any influence, we might expect it to be more a manifestation of effects in other areas of life, especially employment. Girls particularly, when faced with difficulties in the labour market, may replace the goal of a job with that of marriage and parenthood. For boys the desire to get work or at least be financially self-sufficient remains as pressing as ever (Wallace, 1989; Banks et al, 1991).

Against prediction there was little difference betweeen the proportions of married men and women in either the low literacy groups or numeracy groups and the total sample. In all groups married women outnumbered married men in the order of 2:1. Similarly there was little difference in the proportions who were married between the groups of people with self-reported problems and the others.

The results were quite different for numbers of children. Table 5.1 shows the percentages of males and females in the low and high literacy and numeracy groups with different numbers of children. Far more women in the low literacy score and, to a lesser extent, low numeracy score groups than in the sample as a whole had one or more children. Among men there was only a small tendency in this direction. With respect to self-assessed literacy and numeracy problems there was no discernible relationship with having children for either sex.

Table 5.1: Number of children and literacy and numeracy scores by sex.

Number of children	Literacy scores Low	Literacy scores Low	Numeracy scores Low	Numeracy scores Low	All respondents	All respondents
	M %	F %	M %	F %	M %	F %
0	88	62	85	75	93	83
1	10	19	12	18	5	12
2	2	15	3	6	2	4
3+	0	4	0	2	0	1
Total	41	53	96	188	759	864

5.2 Malaise

The 'Malaise' inventory (Rutter et al, 1970) was included in the survey in order to obtain an estimate of cohort members' mental well-being. This inventory consists of 24 self assessment items which respondents either endorse as applying to them (answer 'yes') or reject (answer 'no'). The items describe symptoms which say something about the respondent's state of mind, especially the level of depression they are experiencing. Total scores are calculated by assigning a point for every 'yes' answer that the respondent gives. Scores therefore range between 0 and 24, with 0 being 'very good' mental well-being and 24 being 'very poor'.

It has been suggested that the inventory is a more reliable indicator of mental well-being for females than for males, as the items within it are more in tune with typical female responses to stress than for males. The average score for male cohort members was 3.1 and for females was 4.3. Table 5.2 shows the differences between the various literacy and numeracy groups.

A clear relationship is apparent between well-being and literacy and numeracy. The malaise scores *increase* from the high to the low literacy and numeracy groups. In this case the results of the objective assessments and the self-reports converge. In fact the *highest* malaise scores were obtained by the groups of respondents who reported that they had some kind of problem with literacy or numeracy. This finding reinforces the suggestion in the last chapter that self-reported literacy and numeracy problems are an important feature of overall self-esteem. The malaise inventory demonstrates this more directly by relating

The Basic Skills of Young Adults

Table 5.2: Men and women's mean malaise scores by literacy and numeracy score groups and self-assessed problems by sex.

Group	Men	Women
Literacy scores		
Low	3.9	5.8
Medium	3.2	4.4
High	2.5	3.8
Numeracy scores		
Low	3.3	5.2
Medium	3.3	4.2
High	2.4	3.5
Problems		
Reading	4.0	6.4
Writing/Spelling difficulty	4.4	6.7
Numberwork	5.5	6.7
Total sample	3.1	4.3

these problems to mental health, important elements of which are connected with the self-concept. Those exhibiting most malaise were to be found in the groups with self-perceived literacy and numeracy problems. This was particularly the case among the women who, in any event, had generally the higher scores. It is difficult to escape the conclusion that these problems, or at least the employment and domestic situation associated with them, were playing an important part in the generation of the malaise itself.

5.3 Impact of literacy and numeracy difficulties: self-perceptions

Respondents were asked in the interview if they thought that 'problems with reading, writing and spelling', or 'problems with numbers or arithmetic' had stopped them doing 'as well as they could have done' in their education, training and work and in applying for jobs. These questions were asked as part of a battery of questions about factors affecting career chances *before* respondents were asked about their literacy or numeracy difficulties, and before the assessment was administered.

Only 4% of respondents, said that reading, writing or spelling problems had hindered them in this way, and only 3% said that numeracy problems had had this effect. Respondents who obtained low scores for either the literacy or the numeracy assessment were more likely to be among those who thought that they had been affected. For example, 13% of the low-literacy group said that literacy problems had an adverse effect on their education, training and work, as opposed to only 4% of the medium group and 1% of the high group. A similar but weaker trend was evident for numeracy.

Stronger relationships were apparent with the self-reports. Two thirds of the respondents who reported a reading problem said that the problem had affected their education, training and work and just over a third of those with a writing/spelling problem. Such connections were less evident for numberwork problems. Of those who reported that they had numberwork problems one fifth said that the problem had impeded their progress.

This shows that many respondents with literacy and/or numeracy difficulties also felt that these had affected their lives adversely and that the problem was particularly acute when they perceived themselves to have difficulties. The much weaker links with the objective assessment point again to the significance of self-perceived, as opposed to objective problems, in weakening confidence and damaging self-esteem.

5.4 Courses to overcome difficulties

The data presented so far underline the importance of literacy and numeracy deficiencies in impeding progress in education and employment. In the case of women, particularly, they may initiate early exit from the labour market in favour of having children. We have also seen the damaging effect of perceived problems on the self-esteem and mental well-being of the individuals concerned. How many of these young adults had made attempts to overcome their difficulties by attending special courses designed to help people with literacy and numeracy problems?

Attendance at such courses was rare. Only 3% of all respondents said they had been on a literacy course of some description, *none* of whom were in the low literacy score group. Of those respondents who said that they had a problem with reading, 9% had attended a literacy course and 4% of the writing/spelling problem group had attended a course. Equal proportions of males and females had attended literacy courses.

Attendance at courses on numeracy was only slightly more common; 5% of respondents had attended a course to help them to improve their numeracy skills. There was little difference between the numeracy score groups in the likelihood of attending a course. There was a larger, but still barely significant, difference among those with self-reported problems. One tenth of the respondents who said that they had a problem with numberwork had attended a course, and 9% of the reading problem group as well. Again, there was little difference between males and females.

These figures need to be treated with caution, because it is possible that those who had attended classes would, by definition, have lifted themselves out of the problem group. Nevertheless it is also certain that the figures also point to a large untapped need. It is reasonable to assume that the nine tenths or more of those with problems, who had not attended classes, contained a sizeable proportion who would have benefited from them. It points to the importance of developing better strategies for linking effectively adult literacy and numeracy provision to the people who need it.

5.5 Summary and conclusion

This chapter has shown how literacy and numeracy difficulties impinge on domestic life and psychological well being. The main conclusions are:

- Although early marriage is not associated with literacy and numeracy difficulties, early childbearing among women is associated with them.

- Poor literacy and numeracy is associated with a depressed state of mind, especially in women, and especially when the problem is recognised as such.

- People who report having literacy or numeracy problems tend not to believe that these problems have impeded their progress in education, training and employment although those who have low literacy and numeracy scores were more likely to believe they had been adversely affected.

- People lacking basic literacy and numeracy skills are not more likely than others to attend classes to help them improve their skills; those who perceive themselves as having problems are slightly more likely to attend classes, but the great majority do not attend.

The setbacks men with literacy and numeracy difficulties have in the labour market are complemented by women's exit from the labour market into early childbearing. The objective existence of problems as identified in the assessments may be ameliorated or worsened in its effects by the attitudes people have to their lack of basic skills. Those who perceive themselves as having problems appear not only to have suffered disadvantage in their lives because of them, but appear to have a generally poor self-image as well.

Importantly also, this chapter has highlighted the fact that very few people with literacy and numeracy difficulties attend courses to help overcome them, even when they have identified the problem and believe it has held them back. There is clearly much scope for development of adult literacy and numeracy provision to meet a large untapped need.

CHAPTER 6

Conclusions

Objectives of the study

We started this report with a statement of four objectives that the study had to achieve:

- to estimate the prevalence of literacy and numeracy problems in young adults from self-reports

- to develop an assessment instrument for assessing prevalence of basic skills

- to examine in detail the kinds of literacy and numeracy difficulty people have

- to investigate the background, circumstances and other characteristics of people with poor basic skills.

Let us review what we have discovered about each of them.

Findings

Our survey shows a remarkable stability in the prevalence of self-assessed literacy and numeracy problems over the ten years elapsing since the analysis of 1981 NCDS data for 23 year-olds (ALBSU, 1987). About 12% of the sample reported some kind of literacy or numeracy problem, the most common of which was writing and spelling followed by numberwork and then reading. More young men than young women appeared to suffer from these problems.

An assessment instrument was devised to give a more objective basis to these figures. Using ALBSU's Basic Skills Standards, a number of tasks were designed to tap a range of functional literacy and numeracy skills at different levels. Although the assessment was not a standardised educational test, summary scores have been used, and have proved their worth, as indicators of general literacy and numeracy performance. One of the most pleasing aspects of the study has been the powerful discriminatory power of this assessment instrument. Consistently the assessment has discriminated between those with disadvantaged backgrounds, limited attainments and subsequent poor prospects in the labour market, and those with lives characterised by advantage and success. At the same time, although low literacy and numeracy performance was correlated with the self-reporting of problems, in certain respects the two forms of assessment – objective and subjective – were tapping quite different aspects of the functional problem – a point we return to.

Women performed worse in the assessments than men, which in the case of literacy, could be attributed in part to items which appeared to favour men. With respect to almost all the numeracy tasks, fewer women were able to perform them than were men. The majority of literacy tasks were completed successfully by respondents, which skewed the distributions of total scores towards high performance. However a few items presented problems to quite large proportions of people, especially the elucidation of an argument and the interpretation of a piece of literary text. The numeracy scores were much more evenly distributed, a reflection of the considerable difficulties many respondents found with a large proportion of the tasks. Working out the area of a geometric shape and calculating and using percentages proved particularly difficult tasks, which escaped completely the great majority of women.

Although literacy and numeracy performances were closely related, and in many respects, one formed a surrogate for the other, literacy was the more fundamental. Most people with literacy problems had numeracy problems but a substantial number who had numeracy problems showed no evidence of literacy difficulties. This makes the point that to undertake any educational task, literacy, i.e. the ability to handle verbal symbols, has to be mastered first.

People with low literacy and numeracy scores and self-assessed problems tended to come from unskilled family backgrounds and to have parents whose own educational attainment had been poor. Strong correlations of the assessment scores with respondents' own educational attainment, as reflected in qualifications achieved while at school or after leaving, were evident. The presence of self-reported problems was also related to attainment. People with problems defined either objectively or subjectively, tended to leave education early, frequently to enter training schemes. Women with problems appeared to have done better at school than men with problems, to stay on longer and fewer entered training schemes. However for post-16 educational achievements, women with perceived problems appeared to be at a greater disadvantage than men. Many men in this position appeared to have decided to opt out of education early. But although the women with problems appeared to have remained committed to education longer, once they left school, many went adrift in the labour market, without any clear destination appearing. This was further reflected in experience of unemployment, which was exceptionally high for the young men with low literacy scores. For the young women with low scores or who perceived themselves as having a literacy problem 'housecare' rather than unemployment was common. For many of these young women, opting for having children early was also apparent, even though there was no evidence that they married earlier than the others. Having children bore no connection with literacy and numeracy problems among the men.

Although poor literacy skills, and to a lesser extent, poor numeracy skills, play a crucial role in restricting opportunities for employment, self-assessed problems seem to play a different, but equally important role, in affecting life chances. The significance of perceiving oneself to have a problem appeared to depend on the importance of literacy and numeracy to respondents both at school and in employment. Declaring such problems was to a certain extent a relative appraisal based on the perceived gap between actual skill level and the ideal level to be achieved. Thus perceiving a problem to exist might occur anywhere on the occupational scale. The perception was also often accompanied by other aspects of diminished self esteem, including higher than average levels of malaise and the belief that prospects had been damaged by the literacy and numeracy difficulties. On the other hand, there was little sign of people attempting to solve their problems through attending courses. The great majority of people, exhibiting poor skills or professing problems had not attended literacy or numeracy courses.

Finally as a cautionary note, we need to recognise that these findings relate to 21 year-olds' experience of education and the labour market and domestic life. It is quite possible that later on in adult life, as priorities change, the manifest effect of literacy and numeracy difficulties will also alter. The policy questions that need to be addressed relate to the experience of 21 year-olds and what is needed to improve the prospects of young adults.

Implications

The research has displayed the very serious problems a small but significant minority of young adults have in functioning effectively in the modern British State. If anything our estimates of prevalences are probably underestimates, because inevitably in a longitudinal sample some disadvantaged young people, such as those whose parents had no fixed address when they were growing up or were homeless when we tried to contact them, are missing from it. Without the basic skills of literacy and numeracy, young people are likely to be destined for the least secure areas of the labour market or forced out of it altogether. Their problems are deep rooted, and typically accompanied by an unskilled family background and parents whose own educational attainment was poor. They leave the system of compulsory education without even the key building blocks on which all education and much of employment depends. Clearly to tackle the general problem depends on intervening earlier in life to try to prevent skills deficits developing. The national curriculum may help in this, but the main solution resides with teachers in their responses to the individual child.

For adults the task is clearly massive and needs to be tackled at many levels. The most basic remedial teaching is needed for much larger numbers than are currently getting it. This suggests the need for a campaign to heighten awareness among the potential client population and to bring the teaching closer to them. Such teaching should concentrate not only on the 'core skills', but on psychological aspects of the consequences of not having them. For many students raising confidence and improving self esteem needs to accompany the basic literacy and numeracy teaching. Successful Access programmes depend on this critical shift in self-appraisal even before the step of registering for a course occurs. Engaging adults in the process of raising the level of their basic skills requires first the realisation that a problem exists and secondly the confidence to do something about it. The process involved requires special personal skills on the part of the teacher, the development of which presents perhaps the biggest challenge of all.

Motivating the learner involves convincing him or her that the extra effort required of them to master the basic skills will pay rich rewards in opening up opportunities that have previously been seen as closed. Skills acquired in isolation from the situation from which they are to be deployed may be seen as having limited value. Advice and counselling on further education, employment prospects and assistance in finding jobs are their essential counterparts. This points to a range of educational and occupational services, including the careers service, working together to provide the support the individual needs.

Besides the problems of literacy and numeracy deficits among those who have been severely disadvantaged by them the research has revealed another target for educators. Although in the past poor numeracy may have been less disabling than poor literacy in most areas of working life, in a modern state, this is no longer the case. The failure of large numbers of adults to manage elementary mathematical task points to another deficiency of our education system and the need for remediation on a large scale. Policy makers need to consider how much longer Britain can accommodate such poor levels of numeracy in such large numbers of young adults.

In short the research has revealed a significant problem, explored a little of its origins and pointed to some of its consequences. Much more needs to be done to unravel the complex series of events which lead to basic skills deficiencies. As is so often the case with work of this kind the report raises as many questions as it answers, some of which can be addressed through more detailed and extensive analysis of the data; others await further research. In the meantime there is enough evidence presented here to heighten awareness of the problem. What is needed is the will to solve it.

References

ACACE (Advisory Council for Adult and Continuing Education) (1982) *Adults Mathematical Ability and Performance,* London: ACACE.

ALBSU (Adult Literacy and Basic Skills Unit) (1987) *Literacy, Numeracy and Adults: Evidence from the National Child Development Study,* London: ALBSU.

Banks, M.; Bates, I.; Breakwell, G.; Bynner, J.; Elmer, N.; Jamieson, L.; & Roberts, K. *Careers and Identities.* (1991) Milton Keynes: Open University Press.

Butler, N.R. Golding, J. and Howlett, B. (1986) *From Birth to Five: a study of the health and behaviour of Britain's five year-olds.,* Oxford: Pergammon Press.

Bynner, J.M. (1992) *Transition to Work: Results from a Longitudinal study of young people in four British Labour Markets.* In Ashton, D and Lowe, G. *Making their Way: Comparison between Education, Training and the Labour Market in Canada and Britain.,* Milton Keynes: Open University Press.

Pringle, M.K., Butler, N.R. and Davie, R. (1966) *11000 Seven Year-olds.,* London: Longman.

Rutter, M. et al. (1970) *Education, Health and Behaviour.,* London: Longman.

Wadsworth, M. (1991) *The Imprint of Time: childhood, history and adult life.,* Oxford: Clarendon Press.

Wallace, C. (1987) *For Richer or Poorer: Growing up in and out of Work.,* London: Tavistock.

Sample Design – Scott Montgomery

The BCS70-21 year survey sample was selected from cohort members living in England and Wales, who had supplied SSRU with a current address. In Autumn 1991, SSRU had confirmed current addresses for 8,175 cohort members living in England and Wales. The sample was designed to have the same regional distribution of cohort members as was observed in the population of all BCS70 members living in England and Wales.

A clustered sample design was adopted, based on post-code areas. The post-code area is designated by the initial, non-numeric, part of the code. Twenty-five clusters were selected using interval sampling. An interval of 327 cohort members ($25 \times 327 = 8,175$) was used, where the total number of cohort members available was 8,175. The cumulative total of cohort members living in each postcode area was listed. Postcode areas were listed in geographical order to approximately maintain their relative positions. Starting from a randomly selected point, postcode areas were chosen where they contained each 327th cohort member. If a selected postcode area contained too few cohort members to be viable, the next adjacent postcode area was also included in that cluster.

In order to maintain the original regional distribution, the number of cohort members selected in each of the chosen clusters was proportional to the total number of cohort members resident in the region containing that cluster. Where regions contained more than one selected postcode area, the distribution of sampled cohort members reflected the relative numbers of cohort members resident in those postcode areas. Cohort members were chosen at random within the selected postcode areas.

Table 1 shows the expected and achieved distribution of the sample. Each postcode area represents a cluster, with the exception of E and SE which were combined, as E was selected and found to contain too few cohort members. Once the postcode areas had been selected, additional tracing was conducted to maximise the number of cohort members available in the sample areas. A total of 3,431 cohort members were available throughout the 25 clusters.

Table 1: Distribution of the sample by region and postcode area.

Region	Postcode area	Planned sample %	Interviews achieved
North	NE	6.31	6.24
North West	LA	2.92	2.18
	WA	5.24	5.58
Mersey	L	3.22	2.18
Manchester	M	3.03	3.52
West Yorkshire	WF	4.35	4.55
Yorkshire & Humberside	YO	3.73	3.88
South Yorkshire	S	3.17	3.33
East Midlands	NG	4.12	4.30
	NN	2.54	2.73
Anglia	NR	5.03	5.45
South East	SS	3.98	4.61
	RH	3.59	3.45
	SO	4.53	4.67
	OX	4.83	4.79
	DA	2.69	2.79
London	UB	2.84	3.09
	E/SE	6.24	5.94
	W	2.25	1.88
South West	BH	2.56	2.97
	BS	5.50	5.15
Wales	SA	6.42	5.27
West Midlands	ST	2.53	2.61
West Midlands Conurbation	B	6.57	6.91
	WV	1.77	1.94
Total %			100.00
Total n			1,650

Interview Questions on Literacy and Numeracy

ASK ALL

Q131 **As you probably know, thousands of adults have difficulties with reading or writing at one time or another. It would help us if you could answer some questions about your own experience of reading and writing. Since leaving school, have you had any problems with reading?**

	(21)		
Yes	1	ASK Q132	
No	2		
Can't say	3	GO TO Q141	
Refused	4		21

Q132 **Can you tell me a little more about these problems. First, are these problems due mainly to your not being able to see properly or do you just have difficulties reading?**

	(22)		
Sight problem	1	GO TO Q141	
Just having difficulties reading	2	ASK Q133	22

Q133 **Let me ask you first about some of the problems you have with reading. Can you read and understand what is written in a magazine or newspaper? IF YES: Can you usually read this easily, or do you find some difficult?**

	(23)	
Yes, easily	1	
Yes, some are difficult	2	
No	3	23

Q134 Can you usually read and understand what is written in a letter sent to you? IF YES: Can you usually read this easily, or do you find some difficult?

(24)

Yes, easily 1

Yes, some are difficult 2

No 3   24

Q135 If you have to, can you usually read and understand any paperwork or forms you would have to deal with in a job? IF YES: Can you usually read this easily, or do you find some difficult?

(25)

Yes easily 1

Yes, some are difficult 2

No 3   25

Q136 If you have to, can you read aloud to a child from a children's story book? IF YES: Can you usually read this easily, or do you find some difficult?

(26)

Yes easily 1

Yes, some are difficult 2

No 3   26

Q137 What other things do you usually find difficult to read? PROBE FULLY. RECORD VERBATIM.

....

....

.... 27/28

Q138 When you do try to read something, what do you find difficult? Do you find it difficult to ... READ OUT AND CODE ONE FOR EACH:

	Yes	No	Don't know	
Recognise particular words?	1	2	3	29
Make sense of the whole thing?	1	2	3	30
Concentrate for very long?	1	2	3	31
(Never try to read)			1	32

Q139   **Have you been on any courses or classes since leaving school to help you get better at reading?**

(33)

Yes 1   GO TO Q140

No 2   GO TO INSTRUCTION   33
                                                              BEFORE Q141

Q140   **What type of classes/courses were these?** (RECORD VERBATIM) PROBE

....

....

.... 34/35

ANSWER 'NO' (CODE 3) TO ANY OF Qs 133, 134, 135, or 136 GO TO Q146. ALL OTHERS ASK Q141.

Q141   **How often do you read a newspaper?**

(26)

Every day, including weekends 1

Every day, excluding weekends 2

Several times a week 3

Once a week – weekend editions 4

Less than once a week 5

Never 6   36

Q142   **Now I'd like to ask you about mazagines. In an average week, how much time do you spend reading or looking at magazines?**

Hours   ☐ ☐   Minutes   ☐ ☐   37/40

(37) (38)   (39) (40)

Q143   **Next, I'd like to ask you about books you may have read recently. They might be novels, story books, factual or text books, hardcover or paperbacks, and you don't need to have read the entire book cover to cover. You may have just been looking for some particular information in a manual or an encyclopedia, whether at work or at home.**

Have you read or looked something up in a book during the last six months?

(41)

Yes 1   ASK Q144

No 2   GO TO Q145

Don't know 3   41

Q144 SHOWCARD II. **Here is a list of types of books. Would you please tell me if you've read any of these types of books in the past six months? Which ones?** (INCLUDE COURSE BOOKS ... TICK ALL THAT APPLY). PROBE FULLY: **Have you read any other types of books?**

(42)

01 Fiction 1

02 Recreation or entertainment 2

03 Current affairs or history 3

04 The bible 4

05 Inspiration or other religion 5

06 Science or social science 6

07 Reference 7

08 Manuals 8

09 Cookbooks 9

10 Biographies/books about famous people 0

11 Self improvement books, eg. keep fit, popular psychology X

Other (WRITE IN AND CODE Y) .... Y 42

....

....

Q145 **In an average week, how much time do you spend reading books?**

Hours ☐ ☐ Minutes ☐ ☐ 43/46
(43) (44) (45) (46)

ASK ALL

Q146 **And since leaving school, have you had any problems with writing or spelling?**

(47)

Yes .... 1 ASK Q147

No 2

Can't say .... 3 GO TO Q155

Refused 4 47

Q147   Can you tell me a little more about these problems. Are these problems due mainly to your not being able to see properly, or not being able to hold a pen and pencil or use a keyboard properly, or do you just have difficulties with writing generally?

		(48)		
Eyesight problem	....	1	GO TO	
Problems holding pen/pencil/using keyboard	....	2	Q155	
Both	....	3		
Difficulties writing generally	....	4	ASK Q148	48

Q148   Let me ask you about some of the problems you have with writing. If you need to, can you write a letter to a friend to thank them for a gift or invite them to visit? IF YES: **Can you usually do this easily, or is it with difficulty?**

		(49)	
Yes, easily	....	1	
Yes, with difficulty	....	2	
No	....	3	49

Q149   **Could you write to an employer to apply for a job? IF YES: Can you usually do this easily, or is it with difficulty?**

		(50)	
Yes, easily	....	1	
Yes, with difficulty	....	2	
No	....	3	50

Q150   **Could you fill in a form, from the council for example, or for a hospital appointment? IF YES: Can you usually do this easily, or is it with difficulty?**

		(51)	
Yes, easily	....	1	
Yes, with difficulty	....	2	
No	....	3	51

Q151   **Could you write a letter of complaint about something if you wanted to? IF YES: Could you do this easily, or would it be with difficulty?**

		(52)	
Yes, easily	....	1	
Yes, with difficulty	....	2	
No	....	3	52

Q152 **When you try to write something, what is it you find diffcult? Do you find it difficult to . . .** READ OUT AND CODE ONE FOR EACH.

	Yes	No	Don't know	
Spell words correctly?	1	2	3	53
Make your handwriting easy to read?	1	2	3	54
Put down in words what it is you want to say?	1	2	3	55
(Never try to write)			1	56

Q153 **Have you been on any course or classes to help you get better at . . .** READ OUT. MULTICODE OK.

	(57)	
Writing?	1	
Spelling?	2	
None?	3	57

ASK IF BEEN ON COURSE AT Q153, OTHERS GO TO Q155.

Q154 **What type of classes/courses were these?** RECORD VERBATIM.

....

....

.... 58/59

ASK ALL

Q155 **Since leaving school, have you had any problems with numbers or simple arithmetic?**

	(60)		
Yes	1	ASK Q156	
No	2	GO TO INSTRUCTION	
Can't say	3	BEFORE Q162	60

Q156 **Now I'd like to know a little more about the problems you have with numbers and simple arithmetic.**

When you buy things in shops with a five or ten pound note, can you usually tell if you are given the right change? IF YES: **Can you usually do this easily, or is it with difficulty?**

	(61)	
Yes, easily	1	
Yes, with difficulty	2	
No	3	61

Q157 **If you need to, can you keep simple household accounts of what you have spent or saved or what to put by for bills when they come?** IF YES: **Can you usually do this easily, or is it with difficulty?**

(62)

Yes, easily 1

Yes, with difficulty 2

No 3   62

Q158 **If you need to, can you usually work out what dates go with which day on a calendar?** IF YES: **Can you usually do this easily, or is it with difficulty?**

(63)

Yes, easily 1

Yes, with difficulty 2

No 3   63

Q159 **What is it you find difficult with numbers and simple arithmetic? Do you find it difficult to . . .** READ OUT AND CODE ONE FOR EACH.

	Yes	No	Don't know	
Recognise and understand numbers when you see them?	1	2	3	64
Add up?	1	2	3	65
Take away?	1	2	3	66
Divide?	1	2	3	67

Q160 **Have you been on any courses or classes since leaving school to help you get better at numbers or simple arithmetic?**

(68)

Yes 1   ASK Q161

No 2   GO TO INSTRUCTION

Can't say 3   BEFORE Q162   68

Q161 **What type of classes/courses were these?** (RECORD VERBATIM)

....

....

.... 69/70

INTERVIEWER CHECK Q131, Q146 and Q155:

CODE 1 OR 2 BELOW:

Respondent has problems with reading,
writing or arithmetic
(Code 1 at Q131, Q146 or Q155) 1   ASK Q162   71

Respondent has no problems
(Code 2, 3 or 4 at Q131, Q146 and Q155) 2   GO TO Q165   72

Q162 **Thinking about problems you have experienced with reading/writing/arithmetic, have you always had these kinds of problems or have they come about recently?**

                                    (73)

Always had these problems 1

Come about recently 2   73

Q163 **How often did you receive special help at school for these problems? Was it regularly, occasionally or never?** COMPLETE AS APPROPRIATE.

	Regularly	Occasionally	Never	N/A	
IF CODE 1 AT Q131					
Reading	1	2	3	4	74
IF CODE 1 AT Q146					
Writing	1	2	3	4	75
IF CODE 1 AT Q155					
Number work	1	2	3	4	76

Q164 **I'd now like to ask you about some of the effects these problems have for you in your everyday life. Do they make it difficult for you to . . . READ OUT . . .**

	Yes	No	N/A	
Get a new job if you want one?	1	2	3	77
Cope with a job if you have one?	1	2	3	78
To get on and get promotion in a job?	1	2	3	79
Manage your household business?	1	2	3	80

CARD 24	9

	Yes	No	N/A	
Help children read or learn things?	1	2	3	10
To do the kinds of things you'd like to do in your spare time?	1	2	3	11
To communicate with official people?	1	2	3	12
To get your point of view across when you need to?	1	2	3	13

ASK ALL

Q165 **In general, which of the following did you have in your home, on a regular basis, while you were at secondary school . . . (READ OUT)**

	Yes	No	N/A	
A daily newspaper?	1	2	3	14
A weekly newspaper?	1	2	3	15
Magazines?	1	2	3	16
Comic books?	1	2	3	17
A selection of other books in your home, say 25 or more?	1	2	3	18
An encyclopaedia?	1	2	3	19
A dictionary?	1	2	3	20
A radio or stereo?	1	2	3	21
A television?	1	2	3	22
A typewriter?	1	2	3	23
A telephone?	1	2	3	24
A computer?	1	2	3	25

Time interview finished: ☐ ☐   ☐ ☐   (24 hour clock)   26/29
                       (26) (27) (28) (29)

Length of questionnaire: ☐ ☐   ☐ ☐   30/31
                       (30) (31) (32) (33)

END INTERVIEW AND CONDUCT ASSESSMENTS

Literacy and Numeracy Assessment

Y Number

(23) (24) (25) (26) (27)　　(28)　　(29) (30)

Sample

Most people find some types of reading or numberwork easier to do than other types. Different people have difficulty with different things. We would like to find out a little more about the things that you find easy or difficult to do.

In the last part of this interview I would like you to look at some cards like this (**Showcard AT1**) and answer some questions about them. You do not have to read them out loud to me. You can look at the cards whenever you like – this is not a test of memory. You can take as much time as you like and 'pass' if you do not know the answer. You can ask me to repeat questions, but I cannot tell you if you get an answer right or wrong.

Most people find that they enjoy this. Shall we start?

Hours　　Mins

Time at start of assessment

(31) (32)　　(33) (34)

(24 hour clock time)

Assessment Task 1

Introductory script

I'd like to start by asking you to do some reading. There is nothing to write. Read the advert to yourself and then when you are ready I will ask you a couple of questions about it. You don't need to read it to me.

Instructions to interviewer

Show interviewee the newspaper advert for a concert. When they have read it, ask the following questions:

Script

Q1 *Now you have had a look at the advert, can you tell me where the concert is being held?*

Interviewee answers.

Thank you.

Q2 *Who will be playing at the concert?*

Interviewee answers.

Thank you.

Assessment guidelines

	correct	incorrect
Answer 1: Birmingham National Exhibition Centre (or Birmingham NEC)	☐ 1	☐ 2 35
Answer 2: The Firm	☐ 1	☐ 2 36

Assessment Task 2

Introductory script
This time you have a map to look at. Again there is nothing to write. Have a look at it now and I shall ask you a couple of questions about it.

Instructions to interviewer
Show interviewee the map. Give them time to have a few seconds to look at it and then ask them these questions:

Script
Q2a *Please tell me the quickest route from Oban to Dundee.*
     Interviewee answers.
     Thank you.

Q2b *Is Edinburgh east or west of Glasgow?*
     Interviewee answers.
     Thank you.

Assessment guidelines

	correct	incorrect
Answer 2a: The best route follows the A85 all the way	☐ 1	☐ 2 39
Answer 2b: Edinburgh is east of Glasgow	☐ 1	☐ 2 40

Assessment Task 3

Introductory script
I would like you to do some more reading. There is nothing to write. Look at the page from Yellow Pages then I'm going to ask you a couple of questions. You can look at the page any time. It isn't a test of memory.

Instructions to interviewer
Show interviewee the page from Yellow Pages. Give them time to have a quick glance at it and then ask the following questions:

Script
Q3a *Please could you give me the address of Casper's Restaurant.*
Interviewee answers.
Thank you.

Q3b *What is the 'phone number of Bobby Brown's Restaurant?*
Interviewee answers.
Thank you.

Assessment guidelines

	correct	*incorrect*
Answer 3a: 28 Lower Holyhead Road, Coventry	☐ 1	☐ 2 37
Answer 3b: Leamington Spa 316719 (or number only)	☐ 1	☐ 2 38

Assessment Task 4

Introductory script
Have a look at this advert. You won't have to do any writing. Tell me when you are ready and I will ask you a couple of questions.

Instructions to interviewer
Show interviewee the advert for the Royal Navy. Suggest that they have a quick glance at it and then ask these questions. They need the time to read once they have been asked the questions.

Script
Q4a *What's the age limit for applying, if you are NOT a qualified Engineer?*

   Interviewee answers.

   Thank you.

Q4b *If you want more information, what do you have to do if you make a phone call?*

   Interviewee answers.

   Thank you.

Assessment guidelines

	correct	incorrect
Answer 4a: 26/under 26	☐ 1	☐ 2 41
Answer 4b: Quote reference AF99736/quote a reference number	☐ 1	☐ 2 42

Assessment Task 5

Introductory script

Please have a look at the graphs, which both show the results of the same by-election poll. Again there's no writing involved, simply answer my questions when you are ready.

Instructions to interviewer

Show interviewee the graphs showing results of a by-election poll. When they have had a while, ask the following questions:

Script

Q5a *Using graph B, approximately what percentage of the poll did Labour get three weeks before the by-election?*

   Interviewee answers.

   Thank you.

Q5b *Both graphs show the same results. Why do they look so different?*

   Interviewee answers.

   Thank you.

Q5c *Why would the Labour Party prefer to use graph B rather than graph A to put in an article about their changes of winning the by-election?*

   Interviewee answers.

   Thank you.

Assessment guidelines

		correct	incorrect
Answer 5a:	Approximately 35%	☐ 1	☐ 2 46
Answer 5b:	Differently scaled Y axis on each graph (or answer to that effect)	☐ 1	☐ 2 47
Answer 5c:	EITHER: their support seems to be growing faster in graph B OR: it looks as though they are further ahead of the Conservatives in Graph B (or answer to that effect)	☐ 1	☐ 2 48

Assessment Task 6

Introductory script
I'd like you to have a look at this page from a video manual. There is some text and a diagram on the page. Again you don't have to write anything, just answer a couple of questions when you are ready.

Instructions to interviewer
Show interviewee the video recorder manual. Give them time to read it and then ask the following questions:

Script
Q6a *What's do the initials RF stand for?*
     Interviewee answers.
     Thank you.

Q6b *What is the factory setting for the RF channel?*
     Interviewee answers.
     Thank you.

Q6c *Where in the rest of the manual would you look to find out about the STILL V-LOCK adjustment screw?*
     Interviewee answers.
     Thank you.

Assessment guidelines

		correct	incorrect
Answer 6a: Radio frequency – NOT 'channel adjustment screw'		☐ 1	☐ 2 43
Answer 6b: 36		☐ 1	☐ 2 44
Answer 6c: page 14		☐ 1	☐ 2 45

Assessment Task 7

Introductory script

Please read this passage fairly carefully. You will be asked to look back at it again, let me know when you are ready.

Instructions to interviewer

Show interviewee the article and give them time to read it. Then ask the following question:

Script

Q7   *What are the main points of Jace's argument in favour of hunting?*

Assessment guidelines

Tick all answers given

Answers given can be any of the following:

- bring employment to the area   ☐ 1
- look after the environment   ☐ 2
- conserve wildlife (birds)   ☐ 3
- raises considerable revenue for the Government   ☐ 4   49

Assessment Task 8

Introductory script

I'd like you to read these pages on hypothermia. They're from a First Aid book. When you've read them I'll ask you a couple of questions. You don't have to read out loud.

Instructions to interviewer

Show interviewee the article on hypothermia. Give them time to read it and then ask them these questions:

Script

Q8a *What are the things you could do if you found someone who was suffering from hypothermia?*

Interviewee answers.

Thank you.

Q8b *If someone has lost body heat and become hypothermic slowly, what is the best way to rewarm them?*

Interviewee answers.

Thank you.

Assessment guidelines

Tick all answers given

Answer 8a.

(a) remove outer clothing and replace any wet clothing
     until dry   ☐ 1

(b) put patient in a warm bed   ☐ 2

(c) put a covered hot water bottle under the left armpit   ☐ 3

(d) place in a hot bath   ☐ 4

(e) give hot drinks and high energy food   ☐ 5   50

Answer 8b.	correct	incorrect
The best way to rewarm them is to do it slowly – if they lost heat slowly they should regain it slowly	☐ 1	☐ 2 51

Assessment Task 9

Introductory script
I'd like you to read this short passage. When you've read it I'll ask you a question about it. You don't have to read it out loud. Let me know when you are ready.

Instructions to interviewer
Show the interviewee the passage. When they are ready ask the following question:

Script
Q9   *What was the greatest cause of Jonathon's discomfort?*
        Interviewee answers.
        Thank you.

Assessment guidelines
Answer: EITHER   'The pigeon had routed him'
        OR   'He would not be able to rout the pigeon'
        OR   'The pigeon' *NOT* 'pigeons'

Answered correctly	☐ 1	
Answered incorrectly	☐ 2	52

Interviewer Information

NB. 'ROUT' means 'defeat' or 'displace'. You may accept any answer to this effect.

Interviewer Remarks   (Complete even if test ended prematurely)

Q1   TIME AT COMPLETION OF READING TASK

Hours   *Mins*

(53) (54)   (55) (56)
(24 hour clock time)

Q2   a) Was anyone else present in the room during the administration of this section?

(57)

YES 1   GO TO Q2b

NO   2   GO TO Q3   57

b) IF OTHERS PRESENT: ENTER NUMBER OF PERSONS AND CODE EFFECT
ON COHORT MEMBER'S PERFORMANCE.

EFFECT ON RESPONDENTS PERFORMANCE

NO. OF PERSONS (USE LEADING ZERO)	*Seemed to be harmful*	*None observable*	*Seemed to improve*
ADULTS 58 59	(60) 1	2	3 ....
CHILDREN 61 62	(63) 1	2	3 ....

Q3   a) Was this section terminated prematurely?

(64)

YES 1   GO TO Q3b

NO   2   GO TO NUMBERS SECTION   64

SECTION

b) Reason for premature termination of this section.   (65)

CODE ALL THAT APPLY	Cohort member asked to terminate 1
	Cohort members became uncomfortable and interviewer suggested termination 2
	Major interruption caused termination 3

Other (WRITE IN AND CODE 4) 4 65

MOVE ON TO NUMBERS SECTION

Assessment Task 10

Introductory script

The next part is to find out how happy you are using numbers in a variety of different situations. This first one is about money. I'm going to ask you a question and then I want you to tell me the answer.

You can write anything down if you want to.

You decide to buy two items in a shop. The total comes to £17.89. You hand over £20.00. What is your change?

Instructions to interviewer

Ask the question fairly slowly and repeat it if necessary. If they want to use a calculator, ask them if they can manage without. If they really insist, that is OK, but then tick the box at the bottom of this page.

Assessment guidelines

The question must be right on the first attempt.

	correct	incorrrect	
Answer £2.11	☐ 1	☐ 2	66
The interviewee used a calculator	☐ 1		67

Assessment Task 11

Introductory script

The next questions are to do with time. You can write anything down if you want to. You want to video a concert which is being shown tonight at a quarter to twelve and finishes at twenty past three in the morning. Please answer the following questions:

Q11a *In 24 hour clock time, what time to you program the video to begin recording?*

Q11b *And when would you program it to finish (again, in 24 hour clock time)?*

Q11c *Will a 4 hour tape be long enough (on standard play)?*

Instructions to interviewer

Ask the question fairly slowly and repeat it if necessary. If they want to use a calculator, ask them if they can manage without. If they really insist, that is OK, but then tick the box at the bottom of this page.

Assessment guidelines

	correct	*incorrect*	
Answer 1: 23:45	☐ 1	☐ 2	68
Answer 2: 03:20	☐ 1	☐ 2	69
Answer 3: Yes	☐ 1	☐ 2	70
The interviewee used a calculator	☐ 1	☐ 2	71

Assessment Task 12

Introductory script

You are in a shop and are going to buy these four items. You need to add them up to make sure that you have enough money. You have a pocketful of pound coins and no other change; how many coins will you hand over to the shopkeeper?

OK – here is the list:
£1.40 and £3.86 and £7.15 and 79 pence.

Instructions to interviewer

Show the list to the interviewee. They may ask to use a calculator. Say that you would prefer it if they did it without, but if they really insist, that is OK, but then tick the box at the bottom of this page.

Assessment guidelines

	correct	incorrect	
Answer: £14	☐ 1	☐ 2	72
The interviewee used a calculator	☐ 1		73

Assessment Task 13

Introductory script

This time I'd like you to look at this shape and work out its area. You don't have to do this in your head, and the formula is given. Use a pencil and paper if you like. Tell me the answer when you are ready.

Instructions to interviewer

Show interviewee the drawing of a box and triangle. Make sure they have a pencil and paper. They may ask to use a calculator. Say that you would prefer they did it without, but if they really insist, that is OK, but then tick the box at the bottom of this page.

Assessment guidelines

The answer must be correct at the first attempt.

	correct	incorrect	
Answer: 48 metres squared, or 48 square metres	☐ 1	☐ 2	74
The interviewee used a calculator	☐ 1		75

Assessment Tasks 14 and 16

Introductory script

This task is asking you about credit and hire purchase – HP. You don't have to do this in your head. You can use your pencil and paper if you like and if you want me to repeat a question, I can.

You have decided to buy a car on HP over 3 years paying monthly.

The car costs £4,900. You must pay a 10% deposit.

Q14 *What is the deposit?*

Q16 *Now you have to pay £4,410 over three years, paying monthly. How much do you have to pay each month?*

Instructions to interviewer

Show the interviewee the graphic of the car. Read out the questions slowly. You can ask them a second time if you like. They may ask to use a calculator. Say that you would prefer it if they did it without, but if they really insist, that is OK, but then tick the box at the bottom of this page.

Assessment guidelines

The answers must be correct at the first attempt

	correct	incorrect	
Answer 14: Deposit is £490	☐ 1	☐ 2	76
Answer 16: Monthly instalments are £122.50	☐ 1	☐ 2	77
The interviewee used a calculator	☐ 1		78

Assessment Task 17

Introductory script
This time we would like you to use some charts. You and a friend have decided to go on holiday to Ireland, and you are going to sail from Holyhead. You have to go in August but want the cheapest fare possible for that month.

Q17a *When could you go?*

Q17b *What would be the total* **return** *cost for you both to go in your car?*

Instructions to interviewer
Read out the questions slowly. You can ask them a second time if you like. They may ask to use a calculator. Say that you would prefer it if they did it without, but if they really insist, that is OK, but then tick the box at the bottom of this page.

For question 17b, emphasize that it is the 'return' cost that you want.

Assessment guidelines

	correct	incorrect	
Answer 17a: 19-22 August: 26-29 August (either or both is acceptable)	☐ 1	☐ 2	79
Answer 17b: £230	☐ 1	☐ 2	80
		Card 5 9	
The interviewee used a calculator	☐ 1		10

Assessment Task 18

Introductory script

Look at these two jackets. Both are in the sales in different shops. One was for sale at £200 but is now offered with a 12½% discount. The other was for sale at £250, but now has a third off.

Q18a *What is the difference in price between the two jackets after the reductions?*

Q18b *Which is cheaper?*

Instructions to interviewer

Give the interviewee time to do the calculations. They may ask to use a calculator. Say that you would prefer it if they did it without, but if they really insist, that is OK, but then tick the box at the bottom of this page.

Assessment guidelines

	correct	*incorrect*	
Answer 18a: £8.33 or £8.34 (either)	☐ 1	☐ 2	11
Answer 18b: Jacket B	☐ 1	☐ 2	12
The interviewee used a calculator	☐ 1		13

Assessment Tasks 15 and 19

Introductory script
Have a look at this table. Take a while. When you are ready, I'll ask you a couple of questions about it.

Instructions to interviewer
Show interviewee the table indicating how many people with mathematics A level started on different degree subjects. Give them about half a minute. They may ask to use a calculator for Question 2. Say you would prefer if they did it without, but if they really insist, that is OK, but then please tick the box at the bottom of this page.

Script
Q15 *This table shows how many people with mathematics A level started on different degree subjects. How many subjects had more entrants with mathematics A level in 1979 than in 1973?*

Interviewee answers.

Thank you.

Q19 *What percentage of the total number of students did engineering and technology in 1973? You can give your answer to the nearest whole number if you like.*

Interviewee answers.

Thank you.

Assessment guidelines

	correct	incorrect
Answer 15: 2	☐ 1	☐ 2 14
Answer 19: 25%	☐ 1	☐ 2 15
The interviewee used a calculator	☐ 1	16

Interviewer Remarks

(Complete even if test ended prematurely)

Q1 TIME AT COMPLETION OF NUMBERS SECTION

Hours   *Mins*

(17) (18)   (19) (20)

(24 hour clock time)

Q2 a) Was anyone else present in the room during the administration of this section?

(21)

YES 1   GO TO Q2b

NO 2   GO TO Q3   21

b) **IF OTHERS PRESENT:** ENTER NUMBER OF PERSONS AND CODE EFFECT ON COHORT MEMBER'S PERFORMANCE.

EFFECT ON RESPONDENT'S PERFORMANCE

NO. OF PERSONS		*Seemed to be harmful*	*None observable*	*Seemed to improve*
ADULTS		(24) 1	2	3 ....
	22 23			
CHILDREN		(27) 1	2	3 ....
	25 26			

Q3 a) Was this section terminated prematurely?

(28)

YES 1   GO TO Q3b

NO 2   MOVE ON TO WRITING TASK   28

b) Reason for premature termination of this section.   (29)

CODE ALL THAT APPLY	Cohort member asked to terminate 1
	Cohort members became uncomfortable and interviewer suggested termination 2
	Major interruption caused termination 3

Other (WRITE IN AND CODE 4) 4 29

MOVE ON TO WRITING SECTION

Interviewer Remarks   (Complete even if test ended prematurely)

	Hours	Mins
Q1 TIME AT COMPLETION OF WRITING TASK	☐☐	☐☐

(30) (31)   (32) (33)
(24 hour clock time)

Q2   a) Was anyone else present in the room during the administration of this section?

(34)

YES 1   GO TO Q2b

NO   2   GO TO Q3   34

   b) **IF OTHERS PRESENT:** ENTER NUMBER OF PERSONS AND CODE EFFECT
   ON COHORT MEMBER'S PERFORMANCE.

EFFECT ON RESPONDENT'S PERFORMANCE

NO. OF PERSONS

		Seemed to be harmful	None observable	Seemed to improve
ADULTS	☐☐	(37) 1	2	3 ....
	35 36			
CHILDREN	☐☐	(40) 1	2	3 ....
	38 39			

Q3   a) Was this section terminated prematurely?

(41)

YES 1   GO TO Q3b

NO   2   GO TO Q4 OVERLEAF   41

   b) Reason for premature termination of this section.   (42)

CODE ALL THAT APPLY	Cohort member asked to terminate 1
	Cohort members became uncomfortable and interviewer suggested termination 2
	Major interruption caused termination 3

Other (WRITE IN AND CODE 4) 4   42

MOVE ON TO Q4 OVERLEAF

Final Section: Interviewer Evaluation of Testing Conditions

Q4   DURING THE ASSESSMENTS, HOW WAS THE COHORT MEMBER'S:

	Poor	*Average*	*Excellent*	
a) Attitude towards being tested?	1 .... 2 .... 3 .... 4 5			43
b) Rapport with interviewer?	1 .... 2 .... 3 .... 4 5			44
c) Perserverance/persistence?	1 .... 2 .... 3 .... 4 5			45
d) Co-operation?	1 .... 2 .... 3 .... 4 5			46
e) Motivation/interest?	1 .... 2 .... 3 .... 4 5			47

Q5   DURING THE ASSESSMENTS, WERE THERE ANY PROBLEMS WITH THE
COHORT MEMBER'S:

(49)

a)   Eyesight?   Yes 1

IF YES, SPECIFY _____ (48) No 2   49

(51)

b)   Hearing?   Yes 1

IF YES, SPECIFY _____ (50) No 2   51

(53)

c)   State of health?   Yes 1

IF YES, SPECIFY _____ (52) No 2   53

Q6   DID ANY INTERFERENCE OCCUR DURING THE ASSESSMENT?

(54)

YES 1   GO TO Q7

NO 2   GO TO Q8   54

Q7   CODE EACH CATEGORY BY AMOUNT OF INTERFERENCE

	Strongly interfering	*Somewhat interfering*	*Not interfering/ not applicable*	
1) Noise level	1 .... 2 .... 3 .... 4 5			55
2) Interruptions	1 .... 2 .... 3 .... 4 5			56
3) Distractions	1 .... 2 .... 3 .... 4 5			57
4) Light	1 .... 2 .... 3 .... 4 5			58
5) Temperature	1 .... 2 .... 3 .... 4 5			59
6) Presence of others	1 .... 2 .... 3 .... 4 5			60
7) Others (SPECIFY)	1 .... 2 .... 3 .... 4 5			61

Final Section: Interviewer Evaluation of Testing Conditions

Q8 WHERE WERE THE ASSESSMENTS ADMINISTERED?

		(62)	
Cohort member's residence	....	1	
Other private residence	....	2	
Other Site (SPECIFY)	....	3	62

Q9 WERE ANY OF THE SECTIONS PREMATURELY TERMINATED?

		(63)	
YES	....	1	
NO	....	2	63

Q10 THANK COHORT MEMBER FOR THEIR HELP

Q1 TIME AT COMPLETION OF ASSESSMENT

Hours   *Mins*

(64) (65)   (66) (67)
(24 hour clock time)

GIVE THANK YOU LETTER TO COHORT MEMBER

Showcards

THE FIRM

Appearing at the

BIRMINGHAM NATIONAL EXHIBITION CENTRE

On
19 November 1991
at
7.30pm

Tickets:
£8.50, £10.00, £15.00

6 MAY 1990 — SEE PAGES 6-7

Restaurants—contd.

Berni Inn The, Ansty Rd,Wyken............Coventry 444900
Bharatam Indian Restaurant,
24 Smith St...Warwick 491736
Bhooj-Bhaban Indian Restaurant,
29 Warwick Row....................................Coventry 220671
BLACKDOWN HOTEL & RESTAURANT,
Sandy Lane.............................Leamington Spa 421998
....Leamington Spa 424761
Bobby Browns,
1A Clarendon Avenue.............Leamington Spa 316719

BOBBY BROWN'S RESTAURANT
Open 7 Days A Week
1a Clarendon Avenue,
Leamington Spa   Leamington Spa 316719

Bombay Palace The, 64 Earlsdon St.......Coventry 677851
....Coventry 714057
Bombay Tandoori Restaurant,
38/40 Regent St.....................Leamington Spa 420521
....Leamington Spa 881913

BOSQUET RESTAURANT,
97a Warwick Rd...................................Kenilworth 52463
Both Worlds Restaurant, 10 Henry St........Rugby 76404

Bulls Head, Coventry Rd,Brinklow..............Rugby 832355
Burger Plus, Lower Precinct...................Coventry 223375
BUTCHERS ARMS, THE,
Priors Hardwick,Nr Rugby,Warwickshire.....Byfield 60504
Button Top Roast Inn The,
215 Beechwood Avenue,Earlsdon...........Coventry 714332
Caesars American Restaurant,
24 Victoria Terrace...................Leamington Spa 313432
Cafe Natural, Unit 1 Greenhill St.....Stratford-on-A 415741
Cafe Rendezvous Restaurant,
100 Corporation St.............................Coventry 550145
CARLTON HOTEL & RESTAURANT,
130 Railway Terrace.................................Rugby 543076
....Rugby 550145
Carwardine, 29 Market Way.................Coventry 221805

CASTLE RESTAURANT,
Licensed Restaurant Coffee & Snack Bar
5 The Borough,Hinckley,Leics.................Hinckley 637925
Chambis L, 3 Bishop St.......................Coventry 229696

Chapel House, Friars Gate...................Atherstone 718949
Char Cafe & Restaurant,
36/38 Bedford St....................Leamington Spa 450780
Chatz Restaurant, 67 Station Rd............Kenilworth 511924
City Arms, 1 Earlsdon St.......................Coventry 673008
CLARENDON HOUSE HOTEL & RESTAURANT,
Old High St..Kenilworth 57668
Cocked Hat The, Binley Common House Rugby
Rd,Binley Wood...................................Coventry 440777
....Coventry 458004
Coffee Alcove The,
within C & A Corporation St..................Coventry 222159
Coppice Restaurant (Burton,Middleton
Ltd), 171 Boot Hill,Grendon...............Atherstone 713312
Corfu Restaurant, 1 Heron Way.............Nuneaton 347475

Cottage Tea Shop & Restaurant The,
34 Hill St..Coventry 223642
Cottage The, Southam Rd,Ufton..............Harbury 613184
Coventry Kebab House, 8 New Union St....Coventry 220358
Curry Land, 68 Queens Rd....................Nuneaton 342253
Curry Mahal Restaurant, 4 Victoria St......Coventry 228925

(classification continued)

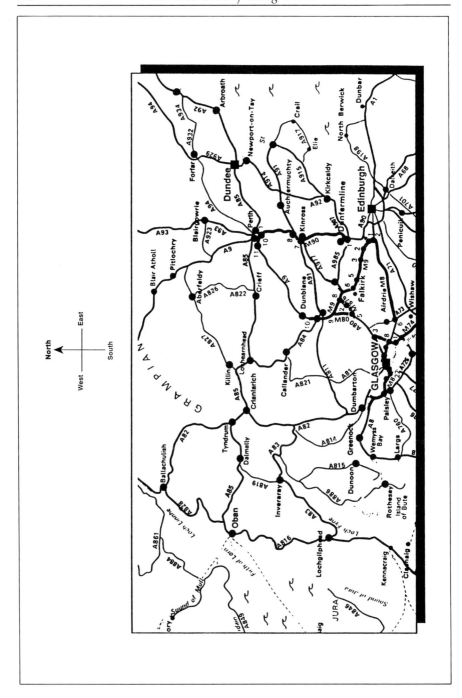

PART NAMES AND FUNCTIONS

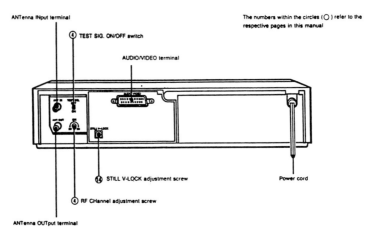

ANTenna INput terminal

④ TEST SIG. ON/OFF switch

AUDIO/VIDEO terminal

The numbers within the circles (○) refer to the respective pages in this manual

⑭ STILL V-LOCK adjustment screw

Power cord

④ RF CHannel adjustment screw

ANTenna OUTput terminal

ADJUSTMENT ON THE TV RECEIVER

Playback signal from the VCR is converted by the built-in RF converter to a radio frequency (RF) for viewing on ordinary TV set. The RF channel can be set to any channels from 30 to 39. The RF channel has been set to channel 36 at the factory. The RF channel should be set to an unused broadcast channel in your area.

1. Set the TEST SIG. switch to "ON" position.

2 Switch the TV to a spare channel or AV button and adjust the TV tuning (channel 36) so that the test picture is clear. If channel 36 is in used by a broadcast station in your area, adjust the RF channel adjustment screw (CH) to select an unused channel from 30 to 39 and tune the TV to that channel.

3 Reset the TEST SIG. switch to "OFF".

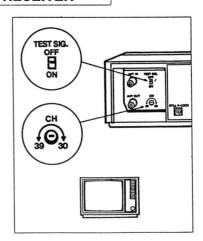

TEST SIG.
OFF
ON

CH
39 30

4

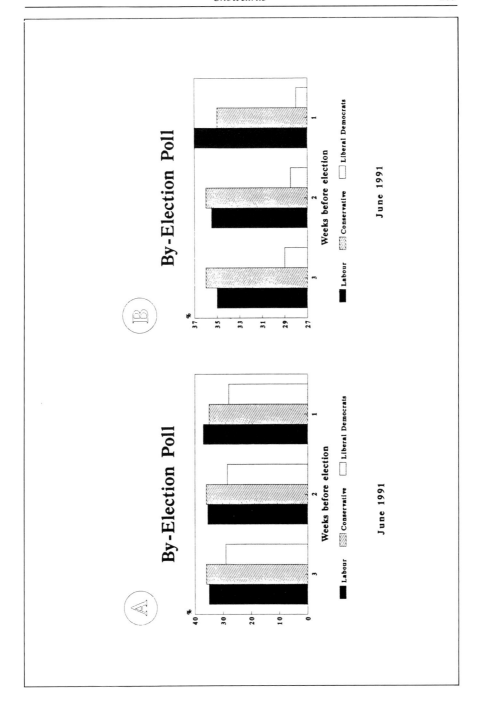

Jace
(a gamekeeper)

What these Anti-Blood Sport Brigade don't realise is the employment hunting brings to an area like this. I mean, you try living here, and I don't mean a holiday. There's nothing to do, we're cut off in the winter. Working for the shoot doesn't just involve a couple of days in August, y'know. We have to maintain the acreage to ensure the habitat of the birds is never ruined and keep the land clean and clear. So in that sense, WE are the environmentalists. We look after the birds, checking for disease and damage, so you see we are conservationists too. Sure we all have guns and I know for a fact, that the licence money on all the guns in Britain brought in over £2 million pounds to the Exchequer. And that's nothing compared to the amount of money hunting, coursing and all the support trades made for this country last year – £22 million in collected taxes. I know if it wasn't for the shoot I would have had to leave here, and it is the most beautiful place in the world.

Did you know that some 62,500 jobs are dependent on country sports. This does not include those casual, seasonal or part-time beaters and pickers up.

HYPOTHERMIA

This condition develops when body temperature falls below about 35°C (95°F). Moderate hypothermia can normally be reversed and recovery will be complete. However, recovery is unlikely if the body temperature falls below 26°C (75°F).

Hypothermia is commonly caused by exposure to extreme cold on mountain-sides or on moors, especially if the cold is accompanied by rain, mist or snow, or by immersion in cold seas, lakes or rivers. Wind chilling also increases the danger.

Hypothermia may also be encountered in poorly heated houses, particularly in elderly people and infants. Lack of physical fitness, fatigue, hunger and dehydration increase the risk of hypothermia. Thin people are more readily affected than fat.

SYMPTOMS & SIGNS

The onset of hypothermia may be insidious and difficult to recognise.
* Casualty may be shivering if in the early stages of hypothermia.
* Casualty's skin is cold, pale and dry.
* Casualty's temperature is subnormal - 35°C (95°F) or less.
* Casualty may behave irrationally and gradually slip into unconsciousness.
* Pulse and respiratory rates are slower than normal.
* As the casualty becomes unconscious, breathing and pulse become increasingly difficult to detect and the heart may stop and require resuscitation.

AIM

Prevent casualty losing any more body heat and help to regain normal body temperature.

TREATMENT

Never presume that the casualty is dead simply because you cannot detect breathing or a pulse.

IF CASUALTY IS AT HOME OR IN A SHELTER

1 Remove the casualty's outer clothing, and replace any wet clothing with dry.

2 Place her in a bed which has been previously warmed.

3 Place a suitably covered hot-water bottle in her left armpit or over her breastbone (this warms the "core" circulation).

DO NOT place hot water bottles at her extremities as this increases blood flow through the limbs, which are still cold, and may result in a dangerous fall in "core temperature".

4 To rewarm her more quickly, place her in a hot bath, at a temperature which is bearable when tested with your elbow (approximately 43°C (110°F). Test the water at intervals, and replenish if necessary. When the casualty's skin colour returns to normal and her pulse rate improves, return her to a warm bed.

5 Give her hot drinks and high energy food, eg., chocolate.

NOTE It is best to rewarm victims of hypothermia at the speed at which cooling took place. A person rescued after falling into the sea should be rewarmed rapidly. An elderly person, or infant who has slowly become hypothermic overnight, should be rewarmed gradually.

Jonathon could not remember ever having carried on such a bungled conversation in all his life. His lies, it seemed to him, were apparent, crudely obvious, and the sole truth that they were meant to disguise - that he would never, ever be able to rout the pigeon, that indeed the pigeon had long since routed him - was most embarrassingly manifest; and even if Madame Rocard had not picked up on this truth from his words, she must certainly be able to read it now in his face, as he flushed and the blood rose to his head and his cheeks burned with shame.

£1.40

£7.15

£3.86

79p

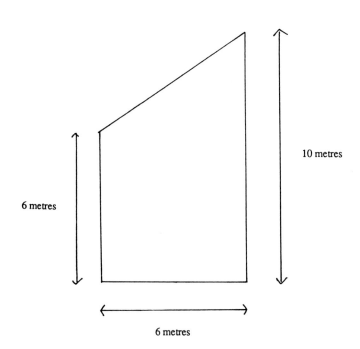

FORMULA

To calculate the area of a rectangle: length x breadth

To calculate the area of a right-angled triangle: 1/2 base x height

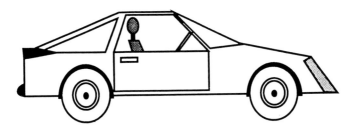

£4,900 over 3 years paying monthly

10% deposit

HOLYHEAD - DUN LAOGHAIRE

Ships: Stena Hibernia Stena Cambria
Check in time 1 hour Crossing time 3 hour 30 minutes

PRICES

	STANDARD SINGLE FARE				
	E	D	C	B	A
	£	£	£	£	£
CAR AND DRIVER	85.00	95.00	115.00	140.00	165.00
MOTORISED CARAVAN / MINIBUS / VAN AND DRIVER					
Up to 6.00 metres in length	85.00	95.00	115.00	140.00	165.00
Over 6.00 metres, each additional metre or part metre	10.00	10.00	15.00	20.00	25.00
TOWED TRAILER /CARAVAN					
Up to 3.00 metres in length	30.00	30.00	45.00	60.00	75.00
Up to 6.00 metres in length	60.00	60.00	80.00	100.00	120.00
Over 6.00 metres, each additional metre or part metre	10.00	10.00	15.00	20.00	25.00
FOOT PASSENGERS / ADDITIONAL MOTORIST PASSENGERS (including car passengers not confirmed at time of booking)					
Adult	16.00	16.00	20.00	22.00	22.00
Child (4 but under 14 years)	8.00	8.00	10.00	11.00	11.00
Infant (under 4 years)	FREE	FREE	FREE	FREE	FREE
SOLO MOTORCYCLE / SCOOTER AND RIDER	34.00	34.00	38.00	43.00	43.00
BICYCLE / TANDEM (rider charged as a foot passenger)	FREE	FREE	FREE	FREE	FREE
DOGS (for domestic purposes)					
In vehicle	FREE	FREE	FREE	FREE	FREE
In kennels	7.00	7.00	7.00	7.00	7.00

IMPORTANT

Please ensure you make a reservation for your journeys to avoid the disappointment of arriving at the port to find the ship full.

STANDARD RETURN FARE

Just add the two Standard Single Fares together for the Standard Return Fare.

CHOICE OF RETURN CROSSING

To travel out one route and return another, add the respective fares for each route to arrive at the return fare.

TIMETABLE   HOLYHEAD - DUN LAOGHAIRE

JAN	0315	1445
	E	E

FEB	0315	1445
	E	E

MAR	0315	1445
	C	C

APR	0315	1445
	E	E

MAY	0315	1445
	E	E
	C	C
	D	D

JUN	0045	0315	0400	1445	1745
		D		D	
		C		C	
		C	C	C	C

JUL	0045	0400	1445	1745
	C	C	C	C
	A	A	A	A
	B	B	B	B
	A	A	A	A
	B	B	B	B
	A	A	A	A
	B	B	B	B

AUG	0045	0400	1445	a 1745
	B	B	B	B
	A	A	A	A
	B	B	B	B
	A	A	A	A
	B	B	B	B
	A	A	A	A
	C	C	C	C
	B	B	B	B
	C	C	C	C
	B	B	B	B

SEP	0045	0400	1445	b 1745
	B	B	B	B
	D	D	D	D

OCT	0045	0400	1445
	D	D	D
	E	E	E

NOV	0045	0400	1445
	E	E	E

DEC	0045	0400	1445	1745
	E	E	E	E
	C	C	C	C
	C	C	C	C
	D		D	

1992

JAN	0045	0400	1445	1745
	E	E	E	E
	E	E	E	E

a= No sailings 11 August.
b= No sailings 8 September
*= See note 5 opposite for altered sailing times on certain dates

Great reductions!

Was £200

Buy now with 12½% discount

Fantastic Value!

Was £250

Buy now ⅓ off

Distribution between subject groups of entrants to degree courses at universities

	Number of entrants with A-level mathematics	
	1973	1979
Subject group:		
Engineering and technology	1500	1714
Physical sciences	1048	968
Mathematical studies	2103	1728
Medical and dental	139	161
Biological sciences	61	47
Other sciences	428	281
Business studies	185	177
Geography	39	19
Other subjects	397	246
All subject groups	6000	5341